Advance Praise for
PERFORMANCE BREAKTHROUGH

"What a delightfully captivating performance! Salit invites us all to be more than we are, to open new vistas for relating with others, and to develop our skills for creative improvisation. And what's more, she provides us with the practical tools for achieving these ends. Given the current context of rapid organizational change, Salit's wisdom is essential."

—Kenneth J. Gergen, author, *The Saturated Self* and *Relational Being: Beyond Self and Community*

"PERFORMANCE BREAKTHROUGH is written in language that sparkles with energy, persuasion, and intelligence. Ms. Salit brings her theater and coaching experiences to life in this book...an instruction manual for any and everyone interested in performing the person they are becoming to the very best of their abilities. I can't think of a business, enterprise, or life situation where the fundamentals of performance as outlined in this book cannot be applied. The illustrative examples and performance exercise manual offer compelling and practical applications of the theories that underlie the benefits and effects of using 'performance' to improve one's performance. And, as a client, I can attest to the effectiveness of the principles that Ms. Salit outlines. This is a book that I will often refer to and reread, and recommend to everyone."

—Sharon Krumm, PhD, RN, and director of nursing/ administrator, Sidney Kimmel Comprehensive Cancer Center at Johns Hopkins Hospital

"What a brave new contribution to leadership thinking! Cathy has a rare ability to completely shift people's view of themselves and their teams, with a masterful touch and a twinkle in her eye. Her work is transformative, and this book captures more than twenty years of experience in a way that is witty, often heart-wrenching, and always practical—teaching us to explore our human potential by seeing through the lens of a director on the 'stage of life.'"

—Tom Andrews, president, SY Partners

"Cathy Salit's PERFORMANCE BREAKTHROUGH breathes life into the tired buzzwords taking over business, education, and social science writing. Here's a book without hype! Bravo! Salit has managed to share not merely her extraordinary successful workplace practice but as well its underpinnings in the theoretical 'breakthrough' of performance as a new ontology. Bravo redux!"

—Lois Holzman, Vygotskian scholar, and co-author,
The End of Knowing

"Performing on the athletic stage is something everyone understands. Cathy Salit surprises us all with her innovative approach and practice about performing every day—off the field of play. She and her team have helped to grow the teamwork and collaboration of our U.S. Olympic athletes, as well as my track-and-field athletes at the University of Maryland. PERFORMANCE BREAKTHROUGH shows us how to harness the power and techniques of performance into achieving our goals in all aspects of life, work, and play. I'm a believer! You will be, too, once you read her book."

—Andrew Valmon, two-time Olympic gold medalist, and
United States head track-and-field coach,
2012 London Olympics

"In a book as energizing as she is, Cathy Salit captures her unique method of learning by connecting what, for many of us, are the exotic concepts of theater with the familiarity of everyday work life. She shows us how to step out of our comfort zones and 'perform' each scene in the office—and life—in new and exceptional ways."

—Linda Tepedino, former VP of
human resources, *Consumer Reports*, and
HR and leadership consultant

"Every CEO—indeed every leader—should read and apply PERFORMANCE BREAKTHROUGH to their business. I will personally be handing out copies of this elegant, powerful book to every leader I know. Wow!"

—Phil Terry, founder and CEO, Collaborative Gain

"Salit and her performance approach is a breakthrough, indeed. She has broken through with new thinking and practices to help business professionals grow and navigate the workplace. In PERFORMANCE BREAK-THROUGH, Salit shares her powerful learning method that overcomes the divide between art and science, cognition and emotion, work and play. Get ready for a journey that is sure to shake and wake you up."
—Judy Rosenblum, former chief learning officer, Coca-Cola, and former president, Duke Corporate Education

PERFORMANCE
BREAKTHROUGH

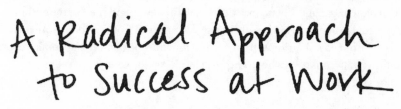

A Radical Approach
to Success at Work

CATHY SALIT

Illustrations by Drew Dernavich

hachette
BOOKS

NEW YORK   BOSTON

This book is a compilation of real case studies and stories, featuring real people from real companies my team and I at Performance of a Lifetime have worked with over the past twenty years. Throughout, I've changed names and in some cases created composites to protect the privacy of our clients. The resulting stories reflect both the wide range of industries and the diversity of the people and teams we work with.

————————————

Hachette Books
Hachette Book Group
1290 Avenue of the Americas
New York, NY 10104

www.HachetteBookGroup.com

Printed in the United States of America

RRD-C

First Edition: April 2016
10 9 8 7 6 5 4 3 2

Hachette Books is a division of Hachette Book Group, Inc.

The publisher is not responsible for websites (or their content) that are not owned by the publisher.

Library of Congress Cataloging-in-Publication Data has been applied for.

ISBNs: 978-0-316-38248-9 (hardcover), 978-0-316-39504-5 (int'l)

For Susan and Murray,
whose performance of life and love inspires me daily

If you hear a voice within you say, "You cannot paint," then by all means paint, and that voice will be silenced.

—*Vincent van Gogh*

Contents

LET'S GET THIS SHOW STARTED

Meryl Streep is amazing. For almost forty years she's filled movie screens with a range of characters and performances that defy categorization and attract awards like nobody's business. When critics write about her work they all say the same thing: Streep "inhabits" these characters and somehow "becomes" them.

And yet, in nearly eighty films (and counting), Meryl Streep has never *not* been Meryl Streep. She never *really* became Margaret Thatcher. She may have looked and sounded a lot like the Iron Lady, but she was, in fact, always Meryl Streep.

Maybe I'm just stating the obvious, but here's the part that may not be so obvious: We *all* do this. We all play many roles. That's what it means to be human and alive. For example: Do you act the same way when you're having a beer with a friend as when you're herding a bunch of unruly kids? When you meet a new puppy as when you're pulled over by a state trooper? No, you have a different performance for each scenario (at least if you want to keep your driver's license).

And that's amazing! Every one of us has the innate ability to inhabit new characters, develop new performances, and make new creative choices as we navigate the scenes of our lives and work. So while Meryl does this with breathtaking talent in front of a camera, the rest of us do it every day, all the time, at work and at play.

But here's the rub: Our performances are usually limited to ones that we've already created. We act in ways we've found to be appropriate to particular situations or circumstances. We have the roles that we play and the scripts that go with those roles. We do the things we do, and creating new and varied performances often seems irrelevant, undesirable, or even impossible. It's not necessarily a conscious choice to limit ourselves and the roles we play, but limit ourselves we do.

My colleagues and I set out to do something about this. We've been helping people expand their performances since 1996 at the company I co-founded, Performance of a Lifetime. We help people in the workplace—from staff to managers to leaders and leaders-to-be—to perform their way to growth, change, and development. We work with Nike, American Express, Coca-Cola, Chanel, PricewaterhouseCoopers, the Johns Hopkins Hospital, DIRECTV, the US Olympic Committee, JetBlue, and the Girl Scouts of America, to name a few. Our method isn't limited to any particular business, industry, or type of work—or to any type of challenge or issue. Our clients come to us for help in doing things they don't

"It doesn't matter what's going on in our personal lives. When we put on this uniform, it's our responsibility to be insane."

know how to do: build a leadership pipeline, become more innovative, increase sales, help high-potential leaders grow into bigger jobs. Whatever the case, we don't help them by addressing issues specific to their industry. We're not accountants, sportswear designers, or radiologists. My team and I are experts in learning, development, and performance; and by helping people to see and act on their ability to perform (new roles, new conversations, new characters, new relationships), we give them a tangible, actionable, consistently effective approach to doing what they don't know how to do.

That's what this book is about, and that's what I'm about to do with you. I'll be your performance coach, helping you to break away from your habitual scripts, take on new roles, enhance your relationships with your colleagues, and grow as a learner and as a leader. In short, I'm going to engage with you as the performer of your work and life. To do this, I'll be guiding you through some pretty out-of-the-ordinary, unusual exercises. But first, let me share with you some of my own out-of-the-ordinary, unusual backstory.

My Back Pages

The first thing you should know is that you're going to be getting advice on how to make your job, your business, and (hopefully) your life better and more productive, innovative, profitable, and fun from someone who dropped out of the eighth grade.

I used to love school. I went to a public elementary school on Manhattan's Upper West Side. It was multiracial, with kids from different economic and ethnic backgrounds, and I had lots of friends. I had a few awesome teachers (Mr. Schwartzfarb was my favorite) who loved kids, loved to teach, and made learning an exciting and joyous experience.

That all changed when I switched schools and entered sixth grade. It was the late 1960s, and the world was in upheaval and changing daily— but this school was not. The curriculum was crusty, as were the teachers. The student body was cliquish and homogeneous. The school was somehow both liberal and authoritarian at the same time. I grew deeply unhappy, frustrated, and confused. Learning and growing, which had been such a joy for me, were gone. Kaput.

My mother was right by my side through this—not just consoling me or helping me with homework or holding regular parent-teacher conferences (which she did), but also introducing me to new ideas that challenged the status quo in education, psychology, politics, and culture. She took me to antiwar protests, civil rights marches, and women's and gay movement meetings and picket lines. The sixties were in full bloom, and a lot of people were asking new kinds of questions, critiquing traditional philosophies, and reconsidering long-held assumptions. What *is* learning? What role does environment play? Where do emotions fit in? What is psychology—a science for "fixing" people? Who decides who needs fixing and what gets fixed? I was only a young teenager, and those questions and critiques were not landing on sophisticated ears, but they still resonated in a deep and meaningful way.

And in the midst of all that depth and meaning, I was doing all the things that teenagers do, including complaining regularly to my mom about school. One day, I came home especially demoralized and upset. A teacher had refused to let a boy in my class go to the bathroom. It was demeaning and horribly unfair, and when I got into a fight with the teacher about it I was brought to the principal's office and then sent home. My mom was there and hugged me tight when she saw my red, teary face. "Cathy Cake," she said (using my embarrassing childhood nickname), "I think we've had enough. How about you quit school and start your own?"

I thought I was hearing things.

But with my mother's help, that's what I did. We found about twenty-five other similarly disillusioned and disgruntled kids who enthusiastically signed on, lined up some teachers who ranged from poorly paid to volunteer, took over an abandoned dry-cleaning shop in the neighborhood, and, at the suggestion of my dad (a creative and savvy adman), named it the Elizabeth Cleaners Street School, which saved ninety-five dollars on signage.

We studied macramé, the history of Cuba, comparative religion, and other sixties essentials. And some calculus and physics, too. And we weren't just students passively receiving an education—we were responsible for everything, from hiring and firing teachers to deciding what we should learn and how it should be taught, to how to best organize the toilet-cleaning schedule. We didn't know how to do any of this. But we did what we didn't know how to do.

We were featured in the *Harvard Educational Review*, and all of us wrote a book about how to start your own school, which was published by Random House. It's on eBay for sixty-seven dollars, but don't buy it. Really.

I don't remember much of what I learned at Elizabeth Cleaners, but it's not far-fetched to say that this experience was the kernel of what would become Performance of a Lifetime. I'm still challenging institutional learning and raising questions about traditional psychology, and I've made it my life's work to not just talk and complain about it, but to build alternative approaches and practices that bring real transformation to people in business, both for-profit and nonprofit, and many other areas of life.

I never did go back to school in a traditional setting, or frankly do much of anything that might be considered normal or traditional. I had gotten my first taste of breaking the rules and making up new ones, and I was hooked. Soon after leaving Elizabeth Cleaners, at the age of fifteen, I enrolled in a teacher training institute for alternative education. My practicum was a school for poor children called the Working Class Room in which I was only two years older than the eldest student.

In my late teens and early twenties, I pursued a career as a jazz singer and composer, then joined a radical artists' collective that founded the experimental Castillo Theatre. In the early nineties we formed an improv comedy troupe at the Castillo. I was a seasoned performer by then, but it was there that I discovered for the first time the incredible discipline, creativity, and joy of improvisation. We evolved a one-of-a-kind show format, in which volunteers from the audience spoke with a (real) psychotherapist onstage, and then the troupe would improvise scenes inspired by the audience members' life stories.

With this unusual show format, we began to see that improvising (performing without a script, making it up on the spot, playing creatively with others) was not only for fun and wasn't always funny. Improvising is an ability that we all have, and it doesn't have to go away when you take your bow at the end of the show. You can step off the stage and use all that creativity and freedom when you get home and when you go to work.

The fact that the other founders of Performance of a Lifetime and I took the road less traveled is precisely why we have been able to help so many people, most of whom have grown up to live and work within traditional environments. I'm far from the first, and certainly won't be the last, to say that the most creative and innovative ideas occur outside of the mainstream. In order to see and act on new possibilities, we need to untether ourselves from things as they are, from the status quo. We have to be free to experiment, to try things and fail, to look like a fool without being overwhelmed by the cultural pressure, politics, and belief systems that tell us *this is the way things are... period.*

Origins of Performance of a Lifetime

Now that you have my story, I want to tell you a little bit more about Performance of a Lifetime, which we call POAL (and we pronounce it *PO-ahl*).

In 1994, as part of my exploration of performance and unusual learning environments, I took a two-day workshop called "The Play Is the Therapy." The program was led by the late Fred Newman, assisted by David Nackman, both of whom were my colleagues and friends from the Castillo Theatre. Trained in analytic philosophy and foundations of mathematics at Stanford, Fred was a maverick psychotherapist, a playwright, and a social activist. David is a Broadway-seasoned actor, improviser, and is now Performance of a Lifetime's creative director.

We participants were pretty nervous in that auditorium. We had no idea what was going to happen or what we'd be asked to do. Fred started by giving a fascinating talk about the relationship between creativity, performing, and personal growth. So far so good.

And then he dropped the bomb. He invited each of us to come up onstage, one at a time, and "perform your life in one minute." The room got really, really quiet. I remember sitting there with my mouth hanging open. How could I possibly sum up, capture, convey my entire life... in one minute? And perform it?! I was an actress and an improviser, but I was still terrified. And excited. And eager. And terrified.

Over the course of the rest of the day, a minute at a time, every one of us gave the performances of our lifetime. People sang, danced, mimed, created poems, played characters. We witnessed every kind of performance you could think of: being born and giving birth, death and survival, emigrating and immigrating, getting married and breaking up.

People came out, ate dinner, heard voices, got and lost jobs, scored the winning touchdown, went skiing and broke both legs, got evicted, said good-bye to their father, and heard their daughter say *mama* for the first time. Every performance was different, and everyone got huge applause.

After our performances, Fred and David gave each of us a directorial suggestion and asked us to perform for forty-five more seconds as a "sequel." Their directions were wild and unexpected, yet they built creatively on the specific performance we gave. *Play your father as a child this time...Do it again, this time in Creole...Sing it as an opera; dance it like a ballet; make it a haiku.* One by one, person after disbelieving person, we did the impossible. The performances and then the sequels were like nothing I had ever seen before. They were honest, deeply personal, and, paradoxically, since they were taking place on a stage in an auditorium, profoundly intimate. Some were funny, some sad, some confusing, but all of them moved us. Each and every one of us discovered, saw, and created something new, for ourselves and for one another, all in *less than two minutes.*

The weekend ended with the 150-person ensemble putting on a sprawling, wildly creative, joyously improvised play that had emerged from the performances of our lives the day before. Afterward, people were buzzing. I overheard snippets of conversation comparing the effects of the weekend to years of therapy, to falling in love, to discovering what the essence of a life was about, and on and on. Somebody said, "I wish I could do this every week."

I myself was completely blown away. It was hard to believe that what seemed like the most chaotic workshop on earth had had such a profound effect. This large group of nonactors was creating theater, on the spot, about ourselves, about one another. Shy and quiet people were belting out songs. Loud and boisterous people were pensive and thoughtful. Everybody was doing something unlike themselves, and at the same time were more themselves than they'd ever been. It was a truly magical experience. But there was a method to the magic. Our directors had uncompromisingly related to us as a performing ensemble—talking to us in the language of the theater, providing direction, creating scenes. Being in this theatrical environment—literally being onstage—gave us the license and permission to do things we couldn't have done otherwise: perform outside our normal roles, play characters that were different from our tried-and-true ones, take risks, share stories, create with others, do the impossible.

I went up to Fred when the workshop was over and said, "This is amazing. You should turn this into a business!" He agreed. So along with David and Nancy Green (a talented writer, painter, and psychotherapist), we founded Performance of a Lifetime. We dubbed ourselves "The Performance School for the Rest of Us" and opened our doors in SoHo, in New York City.

We designed a workshop program where a group of people (most of whom were not professional performers) would go through a four-session theatrical experience, starting with those one-minute performances and improvised sequels and culminating in their presentation of a semi-improvised play we created with them, inspired by their lives.

Our participants loved the program, but with virtually no marketing dollars and a product that was pretty unusual even by New York City standards, our business model left something to be desired. Enrollment in our monthly programs slowed to a trickle, and we began offering a smorgasbord of other classes to keep our loft space occupied and its rent paid.

Things were looking pretty grim around the time of our two-year anniversary when a former workshop participant, a vice president at a financial publishing company, showed up at my office. She asked if we would come and do a workshop with her team, who were having trouble working together in a collaborative and productive way. She thought Performance of a Lifetime could help.

I thought she was out of her mind.

First, if you lined up a group of people from most to least "corporate," I'd be over on the right under the sign reading "least." What did I know about financial publishing? (Honestly, I'm not sure I even knew there was such a thing.) I thought, *I can't do this. I'm a junior high school dropout. I'm an actor, a singer, an improviser. These people will kick me to the curb!*

Second, this was the late nineties (another century), and hardly anyone was doing improv in business back then. What were the chances that a team of financial analysts would agree to something so crazy? *Zero*, I told myself. Nope—I was who I was, they were who they were, and never the twain shall meet. I tried to make these arguments to Ms. VP. She asked me to think about it. When she finally got me on the phone (I had been dodging her calls), she made the winning argument: "I'll pay you fifteen hundred dollars."

Wow. I did some quick calculations on the back of the (unopened) electric bill. This was more money than we had made in the previous month. Sold.

Now the hard part: how to pull it off. I started with costume (an actor's favorite obsession). To research my next character, I went down to Wall Street and watched the businesswomen walk by (a bunch of construction workers and I watched, that is). I managed to put something together from my closet that approximated "the look." And when I walked into that room, I had no choice but to perform as someone who went into conference rooms every day to help financial analysts with teamwork and collaboration. Either that or never open the damn electric bill.

At first, the analysts lived up to my prejudices, rolling their eyes and glaring at me with arms crossed. Part of me wanted to flee the room. But I can be pretty stubborn, so during the first coffee break I decided to choose a different performance—to relate to this team not as who they were (or who I thought they were) but as who they were not—open, creative, and eager to grow.

It worked. And it wasn't that I fooled these people or myself. I actually *did* know how to go into a conference room and help financial analysts build their team. I just didn't know that I knew before I went in there and did it. And they were empowered to break out of their defined roles and try out new performances that were collaborative and cooperative. They were able to change their team dynamics on the spot, to see one another with new eyes, and to have a taste of who they were becoming.

Ms. VP was thrilled, and so was I. Performance of a Lifetime was reborn, and we've never looked back.

About This Book

Performance Breakthrough is a call to action, as in "Lights, camera..."

In this book, just as I did in my early radical days—and have kept doing through our many (still radical) years in the corporate world—I'll help you to create and set the stage, to make use of your natural ability to perform, to throw out your old scripts and try out some new ones. I'm going to push, provoke, and challenge you to get even smarter than you are, to do things before you know how, and to grow philosophically, emotionally, and creatively.

And remember: You don't need acting experience to use the tools I'll be teaching you because we're all natural performers, whether or not we identify as such. You may not yet think of yourself that way, but I'm hoping to show you that you are. So, again, I don't think of performance as something that just happens on a stage or in front of a camera. When I speak in the language of the theater, I'm handing you the keys to the door of a club with a sign that reads "Only professional actors need apply." Come through that door so that all of us can enjoy the benefits and effects of using performance to improve performance.

I've divided this book into three "acts." In Act I we'll delve into the "why." Why performance? Why pretend to be who we are not? This is the most philosophical part of the book, in which I'm presenting a new framework, a new way to see, to be, and to think by embracing our human ability to perform the scenes of our work and our lives.

The second act explores the "what"—the five fundamentals of performance. These comprise the creative and performance building blocks and concepts that will guide you in doing what you don't know how to do. In this act I'll also begin to direct you in some specific new performances, as well as give you exercises that will get you started in becoming who you are not yet.

Act III is the "how," where we'll get down to some brass tacks with stories, practices, and exercises on a variety of themes: how to have challenging conversations, perform as a storyteller, develop leadership presence, coach like a theater director, and expand your opportunities as a salesperson.

One more thing: You may recall management guru and author Jim Collins's guidance in *Good to Great* on the value of a "personal board of directors." It's a great idea. And it leads me to the first piece of direction I'm going to give you: The best way to read and use the concepts, activities, and exercises in this book is to *do it with others*. So do what Collins says—with a POAL twist. Create your personal board of *performance* directors. Let others help you (and you in turn help them) to make performance breakthroughs. Create a personal leadership performance team that practices, learns, and grows together.

And now the overture is done, and it's showtime. So places, please, for the performance of your lifetime.

ACT I

WHY PERFORMANCE?

Who You Are and Who You Are Not

I am always doing that which I cannot do, in order that I may learn to do it.

—*Pablo Picasso*

Henry is seven and got his big-boy birthday bike almost two months ago. But with training wheels, he doesn't feel like a big boy riding it. He sees the other kids on their bikes—smooth and graceful and so grown-up—and wonders what it feels like.

Today he's going to find out, because Mom took the training wheels off. He knows he should be excited, but he's not. He's terrified. How is he supposed to stay up? He doesn't know how to do it. He should never have asked for this, he's not really a big boy, he's made a terrible mistake.

Mom says to get on the bike; that she'll hold on until he gets going. Never, he thinks.

They start down the driveway, and Mom reminds him to pedal. He does, and he feels the bike move a little under his power. He pedals harder and pretends he's one of the big kids on their smooth two-wheelers. Mom's running beside him, and he pretends he's in a race with her. He pretends he's in the Tour de France.

By the time he realizes it, Mom has been standing still for fifteen seconds, and he's riding. Henry's a bicyclist.

———

Cindy is thirty-two and just celebrated her third anniversary with the firm. She's happy there and has done very well, but her boss wants more. She has great ideas, he says, but nobody ever hears them. Why doesn't she speak up in meetings? Because I'd sooner throw myself into a volcano, she thinks. He says he wants her to open next Tuesday's all-hands meeting. She says it's not possible—that she'll panic, forget her words, say something stupid, say nothing. She never says anything. He says he understands, and he wants her to open the meeting by telling a joke. She doesn't reply. He says he'll help, that she should find a joke, and he'll help her get ready.

She goes home, asks her husband for some jokes. A couple of days later in the conference room, her boss listens to her tell one of them. He asks her to do it again, pretend to be Ellen DeGeneres, dance around a little first. She does, and this time he cracks up. She starts to do it again, and he stops her. "Save some for the show," he says.

The what?

She arrives for Tuesday's 9 a.m. meeting at 7:15 and sits in the Starbucks across the street from the office silently muttering her joke. By 9 she's next to her boss in the conference room. He welcomes the team and turns to her. She stands, takes a breath, looks around the room. Takes another breath. And tells the joke.

Then everybody laughs. For a long time. Somebody starts to clap, and then they all do.

Her boss thanks her. He starts to speak. She doesn't sit down. He looks at her.

"I have another joke," she says.

———

When we get up on that bicycle seat for the first time, we don't know how to ride the contraption. In order to learn how, we have to pretend that we do. It's a performance of sorts: Like Henry, we perform as a bicyclist before we are a bicyclist. And by doing so, we become bicycle riders. Millions of people the world over have done this. As adults, when we have a new challenge, when we are being called upon to do something we've never done before, when we need to grow beyond our current capabilities, like Cindy, we can perform our way there. But also like Cindy, many of us are afraid to try.

And that's a shame, resulting in a huge waste of human potential. But it doesn't have to be that way. There's a method for learning to grow, learning how to take on challenges that seem far beyond us, that's rooted in what Henry did—and what you probably did the first time you rode a bicycle. With the encouragement of a caring bystander, you pretended you knew how to ride that bicycle. You performed as a bicycle rider until you became a bicycle rider. Henry (and Cindy) and you...performed as who you were and who you were not, at the same time.

Baby Talk

At one time, you were *explicitly* who you were and who you were not. You may not remember it very well because you were a baby, but here's how it worked: Babies talk baby talk. *Goo goo, ga ga.* Babies do this hour after hour, day after day, month after month. Nearby adults—parents, grandparents, babysitters—respond. They say, "Okay, cute-illy patoot-illy, I'll go get your bottle!" And, "Sure, honey bunny, that's the moon!" And, "Yes, sweetie, that's a bowwow!" Millions of these "conversations" are going on right now, all over the world. And I guarantee you, not one of those millions of adults is turning to the baby and saying, "Listen, kid, I can't understand a word you're saying. Here's a dictionary—learn some language and then we'll talk." No, the adult and the baby are creating a performance. And the adult is relating to the child as both who she is and who she is not—but is becoming. She *is* a baby with no language; she is *becoming* the person who one day will speak words, talk torrents, and maybe even become a CEO. We relate to babies unconditionally as who they are and who they are *not yet*, and in that way we create one of the most successful—if not *the* most successful—performances that people do all over the world and every day of every year: becoming a language user.

And it doesn't stop there. Think back to when you were a kid or about the young children in your life. When second graders run out to the playground at recess, within minutes they're playing characters. They're acting out Mommy and Daddy or the creatures in their favorite cartoons. They have superpowers, funny voices, and in their play, anything is possible. When recess is over, no seven-year-old has ever turned to another and asked, "Was I convincing as Superman?" There's no getting it right or getting it wrong—there's just the natural way that we human beings express our imaginations, by being who we are and who we aren't, and we get a lot of encouragement from the adults in our lives to perform in this way.

I didn't make up this idea of being who we are and who we are becoming. Lev Vygotsky, a Soviet psychologist, formed a theory in the 1920s and '30s around children's language and play that has been very influential to us at POAL and to many schools of psychology and education that believe in the importance of play for healthy development and good learning. Vygotsky's short life (he died at age thirty-seven) overlapped

"I got next game as CEO."

with those of psychology greats Sigmund Freud and Jean Piaget, whose theories have dominated modern psychology. Vygotsky's work laid the groundwork for a different kind of psychology but, suppressed by Soviet rule, it was virtually unknown there, or anywhere, until the 1960s.

Vygotsky believed that humans, being essentially social animals, achieved growth by engaging in group activity with other humans (e.g., all that goo-goo-ga-ga talk that we grown-ups respond to as if it makes perfect sense) rather than through an individual, internal process driven by our responses to external stimuli. We don't, according to Vygotsky, grow, change, evolve, and transform by having things happen *to* us; we *create* growth, change, and personal evolution ourselves by engaging in our culture's activities *with those around us*. Rather than learning and growth happening individually and as an internal process, human beings learn and grow through and with others.

Vygotsky's brilliant work and study didn't extend beyond childhood. But a new crop of psychologists and educators have taken his work further to include adult learning and development, and today the research and study of how play, performance, and development are related is a burgeoning field sometimes called performative psychology, of which Vygotsky and Performance of a Lifetime are a part.

Welcome to Adulthood

Eventually the encouragement we received as children—as well as most of our performing—dissipates. There's that point in most of our lives when we go from being praised for trying something new (even if we didn't get it right) to being told we didn't get it right (even though we were trying something new). Maybe we bring home a drawing and expect it to be proudly displayed on the refrigerator. But instead of the "ooh" and "aah" we're used to, our parents say, "That's not a horse! A horse doesn't have toes!" Maybe we go from loving soccer to not being good enough to join the team. Or we get told that if we keep making that face, it'll freeze that way.

People stop growing and developing precisely because they no longer take part in the kinds of performances that encourage them to be—in Vygotsky's words—"a head taller" than they are. In environments that expect adults to do only what they already know how to do (as well as environments that demand that we do what we don't know how to do and provide no way to learn it), we are not likely to take risks to perform as other than who we think we are. Instead, we tend to repeat our well-learned patterns and passively play out the roles we have already learned and are comfortable with.

We play it safe because more and more we get the message: Color inside the lines; know the correct answer; understand how to behave and fit into society. And a lot of that's pretty important—we need to learn how to safely cross the street, tie our shoes, calculate a tip, and about a billion other things. But as we grow into adults, this need to *get it right* eventually takes over. We put a lot of effort into it, and we get rewarded for it. We learn what we need to in school and then at our jobs. There's little support to create new performances. Getting it wrong, not knowing something, experimenting, trying something new, being silly, and making a fool of yourself are in most spheres of adulthood flat-out discouraged and usually disdained. We become expert at being who we are—as defined by ourselves and others—and in that box there's not much room for development, growth, or testing out new waters.

On top of these definitions, throughout our careers we are often given tests to help us (and our employers) specify, identify, and narrow even further who we are. From Myers-Briggs to Wonderlic, these instruments can provide many interesting insights. But when insight becomes definition—if you're an ESTP, you're a Doer; if you're an INTP, you're a Thinker (because everyone knows you can't be a Thinker and a Doer)—we start acting more like this tiny collection of letters we've been assigned. These definitions are antithetical to change, to growth, to transformation, to becoming who we are not...yet.

The fact is, we can all grow and develop as adults. That is, we can reinitiate the kind of creative learning and development experiences and abilities we had as children so that we can perform in new ways, do new things, and break out of habitual scripts that are holding us and our organizations back. We are in plays of our own making, as well as in the plays of others. As performers in life and work, we can impact these plays in a rich variety of ways. We can exercise our human ability to change our performances.

We call this approach The Becoming Principle™, and it's an unusual blending of theater and improvisation, together with breakthroughs in the human development sciences, that makes it possible for individuals, teams, and companies to learn, grow, and develop and do things before they know how. Sometimes that means becoming what and who you want to be. Sometimes it means discovering a way to be that would never have occurred to you.

The Becoming Principle in Action

Let's take a common workplace challenge: improving interpersonal and relationship building skills. It's critical to any role, from the C-suite to the factory floor, from leadership and teaming to sales and customer service. It's also a lot like the challenge we all faced as babies when we were learning to speak—just as the dictionary wouldn't have been much help to us then, a cognitive approach to better interpersonal skills falls short now, and in a very important way. It's simply not possible to think and analyze your way into the social activity of relationships. To get better at them, you have to *perform* them, *with others*.

So when a global electronics company asked us to work on this skill with their highest-potential leaders, we introduced a set of performance experiences that are at the heart of building relationships. Here's one example: Two people face each other. Their job is to mirror each other's movements simultaneously—in complete silence. When one slowly moves his arm or tilts his head, the other has to perform as the mirror and move in exactly the same way, at exactly the same time. It's much easier said than done, and, at first, there is usually a big gap between the movement of one person and the other.

But by practicing this exercise for even a few minutes, people start to learn to perform a relationship in a new way. If one of the pair isn't able to follow the other, who is responsible? People in leadership or sales roles immediately grasp that they need to notice whether they are making it possible for someone to follow them, to collaborate, to connect; that it is not the follower's responsibility to "catch up" and get with the program. In the exercise, with a little bit of coaching and practice, they learn to slow down and focus on the other. They see/feel/experience what it means to be in sync with their colleagues or customers. That way of performing is learned and remembered in their bodies, not memorized from a list of do's and don'ts.

Here's another example of the Becoming Principle in a difficult, high-stress situation: Imagine you are the nursing supervisor at a world-renowned cancer center. You're part of a hopeful organization, developing and administering cutting-edge treatments not available elsewhere. Your nurses are dedicated to their jobs, working long hours caring for (and becoming attached to) their patients. But as with oncology units everywhere, they burn out and quit their jobs more quickly than any other type of nurse. The pain of repeated death can be too much to bear. Can you help them learn to bounce back more easily and be nourished by their work?

When the director of oncology nursing at a major hospital brought us in to work with her 250 nurses, we got them performing right away. We asked them to perform scenes of their work in brief improvised skits together: talking to a nineteen-year-old patient dying of leukemia, or being a nineteen-year-old patient dying of leukemia. They were always moving performances—sad, funny, shocking, deeply personal—and always challenging to perform.

Performing onstage with and for one another allowed the nurses to see the variety of performance choices they were making. Some of these were nourishing, and some were hurtful and draining. The question we set out to answer was: What performances were needed for the nurses to become more resilient? Together we discovered that most nurses did not know how to ask for help—from one another, at home, pretty much anywhere. By training and disposition, they know how to care for patients but not for themselves or one another. In their onstage scenes, we saw how challenging it was for a nurse to say, "I'm tired—can you help me turn this patient's bed?" Or, "I can't sleep. I miss my patient so much, and I'm so upset I couldn't save him." But by speaking these "lines" in a "rehearsal" environment, the nurses began creating a new play—with new characters, new scripts, and new ways to relate to one another. In these new performances, they were who they were (stressed out, upset, sleep-deprived) *and* who they were becoming. They learned how to ask for and to give help by performing in scenes in which they asked for and gave help. And, immediately, that new rehearsal/play began to create a support system that helped produce greater resiliency and continues to this day.

Performance can, indeed, have a profound effect on performance.

To Become or Not to Become

If performing—being who you are and who you are becoming—sounds weird, counterintuitive, and not worth the risk, think about this: In most workplaces, we can no longer thrive and grow by seeing, thinking, and acting only within the status quo or what's "normal." In the workplace, the marketplace, our personal lives, politics, and culture, our world continues to change and transform. Billions of words have been spoken and written about how rapid change is the new normal. To get better at navigating that change, we need to develop tools for new ways of seeing, understanding, and participating in creating that change. We can't stand still, personally or professionally.

I once heard the Pulitzer Prize–winning poet Stanley Kunitz read from his poem "The Layers," which ends with the line "I am not done with my changes." He was ninety-seven when I heard him say that. Clearly, we *all* can become who we are not yet.

So what will your new performances (of you) be? Maybe it's performing new ways of conducting or participating in the Thursday morning staff meeting, the sales pitch with a client, the performance review, the promotion that got you a new seat at a new table. Who (and how) will you become? There's only one way to find out: Let's get onstage.

All the World's a Stage

All the world's a stage,
And all the men and women merely players.
They have their exits and their entrances,
And one man in his time plays many parts.
                                        —*William Shakespeare*

I'm sure you've heard at least the first part of this quotation. Maybe you've even seen *As You Like It*, the play it's from. For those of you who haven't, indulge me in a quick plot synopsis:

Oliver is rich, privileged, and (through rotten aristocratic parenting) has grown up to be a very bad dude. Among other dastardly doings, he torments his younger brother Orlando and banishes him to the forest just as little bro has found true love with the fair Rosalind. Not to be thwarted, Rosalind and her BFF Celia go undercover and head into the woods to find Orlando. Rosalind tracks down Orlando and, disguised as "Ganymede" (a shepherd and manly man), assures the lovelorn exile that "he" will help Orlando win back his ladylove (who is, of course, actually Ganymede aka Rosalind). Then it gets complicated. Another dozen or so characters get involved, among them Phebe, a humble shepherdess who falls in love with "Ganymede." Oliver repents his nasty ways and falls madly in love with Celia, who's disguised as the lowly peasant "Aliena." There is much confusion about who will marry whom, which Rosalind/Ganymede promises to resolve. In the end, the lovers reveal their true identities and get married. And all's well that ends well.

The changes in *As You Like It* are dizzying—changes in gender, status, love interest, character, facial hair, you name it. Putting on a new hat and jacket transforms a woman into a man; an aristocrat into a peasant; a woodland crush into a husband or wife. And, of course, in Shakespeare's day, all the roles were played by men. So in *As You Like It*, first you had a man playing the role of Rosalind, a woman. Then Rosalind, the character played by a man playing a woman, changes herself/himself into a man. Then back again into a woman played by a man.

It's not just that the characters go through changes in *As You Like It*; one of the fundamental principles of theater is that it is an ongoing, creative, and transformative art form. You've probably read articles or heard actors and playwrights and directors speak about the life-changing experiences they had working on a particular play, or character, or movie, or scene. For actors, the opportunity to play someone other than themselves helps them to see, feel, and experience human life in new and different ways. A playwright creates characters with attitudes, points of view, and life stories completely different from her or his own and then, as the writing process unfolds, experiences these "strangers" speaking and acting in ways the writer would never have imagined. Directors begin with a vision of the production and then immediately begin working creatively with an amazing combination of inputs: the cast, the playwright, the characters, the props, the costumes, the physical environment, and more. When this process of collective and chaotic creativity works, the final product transcends the individual vision of any of its contributors, transforming everyone in the process.

Let's Get Real

But is *all the world* really a stage? And are *all the men and women* really players? Here at Performance of a Lifetime, our answer is a resounding *yes!* Obviously most of us will never be in *As You Like It*. But as I've said, we're all performers, and each and every one of us plays different characters and performs differently according to the scene and the environment we're in. What happens when you see a little kitten? For most of us, our voice gets high and we might even start to squeal, "Hello, wittle kitty. You're the cutest thing I've ever seen!" Now, you don't always talk that way, but it wouldn't be accurate to call you a liar because that's what and how you spoke to that little bundle of adorableness. And obviously, when greeting your CEO, you wouldn't say, "Hello, wittle Cynthia. That was the cutest strategic report you gave this morning." That would probably get you fired, or at least a psych evaluation. No, you'd have a completely different performance in that scene, as different as the one when you get into your car, blast the music, and start rocking out while you drive. Or your performance as you sit meditatively in the park or on a mountain. Each of these performances makes sense for the scene and the play you're in.

Every moment of every day, you're making performance choices based on who you are, where you are, and who you're with (including when you're by yourself). You make performance choice after choice after choice, changing characters seamlessly, without necessarily even realizing you're doing it. Many of these performances don't feel like choices at all. Sometimes our performances become scripted and habitual— so habitual that we don't even notice them. But they are performances nonetheless. *Everything* you do is a performance.

Enter a Leader

Natasha had recently been promoted to report directly to the global head of her department at a financial services company. Her span of control had doubled in size, and she had a whole new set of relationships to manage. But her boss, Jorge, said Natasha wasn't consistently showing up as the leader he needed her to be. "I don't think she sees that how she shows up *everywhere* matters now," he said, "whether that's walking into the elevator and making small talk or participating in one of my leadership team meetings."

My colleague, POAL's awesome managing partner and performance coach and director par excellence, Maureen Kelly, asked Natasha to describe a few situations she's regularly in, using the language of the theater: Who are the *characters* she's performing with, what's the *scene* (where the action takes place), and what is the *purpose* of that scene in the overall business play? And to get at the crux of their work, Maureen asked Natasha to describe her own *leadership character*, as well as her *objective* in each scene.

One recurring scene was a town hall meeting, in which Jorge and members of the leadership team update the organization on quarterly results. Jorge leads the meeting, and Natasha and her peers are the supporting cast. "This is a scene I often feel awkward in," she said. "There's mingling beforehand, there's the Q-and-A, and then mingling after." Natasha didn't have an official speaking role, so she tended to fade into the background.

Maureen posed some questions: What kind of leader did she want to be in this scene? What did the town hall scene need more or less of? What did Jorge need from her? Natasha thought about it. "Well, I have this one colleague who *always* has something to say during Q-and-A—he just talks to talk. Drives me crazy. I *know* I don't want to be 'that guy.'"

Natasha knew who she *didn't* want to be, and it was keeping her silent. Maureen swiftly pulled together a powwow with Natasha and some of her colleagues who knew her well to get some collective direction. At first Natasha was a bit freaked out. "Maureen, I don't want to impose on them! And—what if they say something I don't want to hear?" Maureen reassured her that they had already signed on as part of her personal board of performance directors (remember, from the introduction?), and based on the work her colleagues and she had done with POAL earlier, Maureen felt certain they would support her on this.

Natasha acquiesced, and her teammates were ready to help. They shared their impressions of Natasha, and what quickly emerged was that they saw her as a great "translator." She was, they said, highly skilled at giving concrete, on-the-ground examples of Jorge's strategy and the organization's success. When he heard this, Jorge agreed wholeheartedly. "Let's make it official," he told Natasha. And then (trying on the language of theater himself) he said, "Perform as my strategic partner and translator. Have my back and the team's back."

At the next meeting, Natasha tried out her new translator character. After Jorge gave a high-level overview of a new project, Natasha followed up and named the folks who were key in the rollout, and she talked about how well it was going and some of the interesting challenges that the team was taking on in the process. She invited some of the team to share specifics and then connected those back to the high-level strategy that Jorge had laid out. When she spoke with Maureen later, she was thrilled. "This role freed me up," she said. She found that she actually had quite a lot to say. She was able to bring others into the conversation and was, in her own words, "on fire." "I'm not obsessively thinking about myself," she went on. "Well, I'm not *only* thinking about myself! Ha! I found my character and my objective, and I have a performance to give as a leader in that room."

Natasha savored her victory and was ready for more, so Maureen dug deeper. Recalling Jorge's comments about Natasha needing to show up as a leader not just in formal settings but everywhere, she asked Natasha to describe some of her less obvious leadership scenes.

Natasha started at the top of her day, and they soon found their next scene to redirect. It turned out that Natasha came into work in the morning with her headphones on, eyes often focused on her iPhone, not making eye contact, distracted and far away in the back of the elevator. She said she had never thought about what she looked and acted like when, as she put it, she's "not even at work yet."

What Natasha didn't see was that she had already entered the stage of her office long before she stepped onto her floor. She and Maureen examined her entrance more closely, and she realized that she was onstage from the moment she walked off her commuter ferry and stepped onto the crowded street a quarter mile from her office. There were colleagues surrounding her from that point on—Natasha had just never acknowledged them before. Whenever someone approached her, she always felt surprised, taken off guard.

So Maureen had Natasha make some new, small performance choices. While on the commuter ferry she enjoyed the breeze, her music, and the water. But as soon as she walked the plank (pun intended) to the pier, she got into character. She took off the headphones, said hello to fellow employees on the way to the office, and smiled at people in the elevator. Each of these choices transformed Natasha from the *leave-me-alone-don't-bother-me-yikes-who-are-you-anyway!?* gal to the ready-to-go business executive that she was. After a few days of performing her entrance this way, Natasha told Maureen, "What's funny is that I notice that when I go 'into my head' on the walk, often what I'm thinking about are the particular meetings I have with people that day—and it kind of stresses me out. Now I'm seeing opportunities to be friendly, engage with people, or simply take in my surroundings. It's way more relaxing."

Behave Yourself or Perform Yourself?

While it may sound like I'm using the word *performance* as a metaphor, I'm not. (Sorry, Erving Goffman.) Nor am I using the word *performance* to describe something above and beyond what might be considered normal human behavior. While *behavior* is a word that can describe what every animal does, *performance* is a word that can describe what only humans do. Performance, to me, isn't a "kind" or "subset" of human behavior. What I'm saying is that performance is a substitute for the whole idea of human behavior. For this reason, I see performing as integral to the essence of our humanity.

Some of our performances are extraordinary and beautiful (a carefully composed eulogy for a loved one, helping deliver a baby, landing an engineless plane on the Hudson River). Some are hard for us (ending a relationship, caring for an aging parent); some are habit (smoking, brushing our teeth, muttering hello when we come home to our partner of ten years). Some performances are run-of-the-mill (walking the dog); and some are shockingly ugly (hurting a child). Some are rehearsed, some improvised, and some a combination of the two.

We humans are, by our nature, performative. As we've discussed, babies and children do it all the time. And here's some very good news: As adults, we can now go much further as performers. As babies and kids, we weren't conscious that we were performing. It's just what we did. As adults, however, in order to keep growing and changing, we have to become conscious of what we do naturally. Vygotskian scholar Lois Holzman, a close friend and mentor to me, helped me to understand this with a great analogy. "We're breathing all the time," she told me. "And we usually don't pay any attention to it. But sometimes we're instructed to breathe, like in yoga. When we add that awareness to our breathing, it becomes possible to breathe in different ways. If you sing, run, meditate, swim, practice yoga, etcetera, you're doing a different breathing performance."

And so it is with performing in everyday life and work. We're taking this beautiful, natural, and uniquely human activity and making it conscious, in all its complexity. We can both be in a scene and see it unfold; we can write, perform, and direct it simultaneously. We can be fully engaged in a conversation with a colleague, a client, or a loved one, *and* have a point of view about how the conversation is going, *and* make creative choices that impact the scene, the characters, and the relationship—*all at the same time.*

Yes, all the world *is* a stage. And we have a word to describe what makes that world go 'round. It's our amazing, creative, and unique ability to *perform.* Behavior doesn't come close.

"You'll find that Linda has a flair for the dramatic."

Be More of Who You Are by Performing Who You're Not

Bright, very technical, and a bit of a "quant," Nicholas was on the brink of big things. An analyst at an oil and gas company, he was having trouble coming up with the kind of breakthrough performance that would let people know he was ready for his next promotion.

Nicholas made a lot of presentations—to clients, his bosses, and colleagues. He told me he thought he was a competent speaker but that he had room for improvement. He was right. He almost never smiled, had trouble making eye contact with an audience, and his sense of humor—so apparent when we were one-on-one—was nowhere to be found, making him seem a bit wooden. We decided to work together on his next presentation, which was to a group of new hires.

I began by giving him some of the usual directions and techniques that pretty much any public-speaking coach would give: Slow down, remember to make eye contact, smile more, and then practice to make those things more relaxed and natural. It was all helpful. He had taken my tips to heart, and he was dutifully making baby steps toward a better presentation style. But to go beyond baby steps and make the kind of leap that would allow *all of him*—his passion, creativity, sense of humor, and smarts—into his performance, well, that was uncharted territory. I decided to give Nicholas a big performance challenge.

One of his bosses is a vice president in the company. His name is Scott, and I've met him and like him a lot. Scott is a great talker and an incredible salesperson. He's such a good salesperson that sometimes he can verge into used-car territory. He's an arm grabber and a world-class schmoozer. So when I proposed to Nicholas that he *perform as Scott*, I suspected he'd have a big reaction, and he didn't disappoint. He looked like he was going to throw up.

"You're out of your mind," he said. "Scott is the *opposite* of me."

"I know," I said.

"I can't do it. I won't."

"Look," I said, "I guarantee you, you're not going to *turn into* Scott. Just perform *as* him."

There is a method behind this madness. I needed to get Nicholas out of his head and away from the cognitive thinking, planning, and worrying about *what* he was saying and into the performative *how* he was saying it. We all know the axiom that to grow you have to get out of your comfort zone. I knew I needed to get Nicholas out of his in order to discover what he didn't know he was capable of doing until he got there.

So I did what any self-respecting mad scientist of developmental performance would do—I turned to our friend Lev Vygotsky and his idea of "performing a head taller." For Vygotsky, one of the key ways children accomplish this performance is by imitating—not parroting in a mechanical way but performing as someone or something that's beyond them. Performative psychology calls this "creative imitation," and it would be just the thing for Nicholas. He needed a model, someone who was better at talking to people than he was, someone whom he could creatively imitate. And that creative imitation couldn't be too easy for Nicholas to do (we're going for a "head taller" here, not a nose or a pinkie). But it also couldn't be Winston Churchill or Steve Jobs or some other great speaker whose skill and subject matter were completely out of reach.

That's what I was thinking about as I applied my powers of persuasion and got Nicholas's agreement to perform "as Scott" (though I confess, his agreement looked suspiciously like stony silence). We started to rehearse. He took a minute to get into character, and then...the skies opened up! He stopped reading the massive blocks of fine print on the

PowerPoint and told a story instead. He rolled up his sleeves while smiling and asking questions of the imaginary audience (that's me, moving around from seat to seat and playing different people). He was smart, quick, and charming. He had a gleam in his eye. Nicholas's personality was shining through. In fact, a Nicholas that I didn't even know existed surfaced during this rehearsal.

Nicholas wasn't so sure. He felt like he was overdoing it.

"No!" I practically yelled at him. "You're still you! You're not Scott. You're actually a more animated, interesting, captivating version of Nicholas."

He had a choice to make, and I give him a lot of credit for what he did next. Nervous as he was, he took the risk and did his presentation as his stylistic arch-nemesis, Scott. The result? Another one of Nicholas's bosses, who was himself a very good speaker and had a pretty high bar, simply said, "He knocked it out of the park. It couldn't have been better." A very senior VP said, "I've heard more presentations of technical material than I care to remember, most of which I don't get. Today was the first time I understood the material and actually found it interesting, because Nicholas was so compelling, because he told great stories, and because he was so enthusiastic."

Soon after, Nicholas got his promotion. In an ironic end to the tale, Scott, the Super Salesman, asked Nicholas to come work for him exclusively, which was exactly the kind of opportunity that Nicholas needed to continue to grow his career. And I loved Nicholas's reaction to Scott's offer, which he told me shortly after hearing the news: "Scott is a great guy. I have a lot to learn from him."

Playing Roles and Breaking Out of Roles

When we look at ourselves and the world through the lens of the Becoming Principle (from the perspective of a performer), it becomes clear that we can play an astonishing variety of roles and act in a breathtaking variety of plays. We can write new lines for ourselves, we can wear new costumes, we can change the set, we can direct ourselves to react to people and situations in completely new and different ways.

When people stop growing and developing, often it's not because they don't have the ability or desire—it's not that they've reached some kind of limit to their adaptability and flexibility. It's more that they've stopped performing in ways that make it possible for them to change and grow. We spend our lives acting out roles that have been given to us or that we've picked on the basis of environment, gender, background, social class, ethnicity, or age. Frustratingly, once we've adopted these roles, the developmental process that got us comfortably (or uncomfortably) into the roles tends to shut down altogether. Strangely and sadly, when we become adults and leave behind the idea of playing and pretending, we typically stop developing. But by getting back into the kid space (as adults), where we can play, pretend, and perform, we create the conditions for lifelong learning and development. We can perform as—and become—who we're not yet. Which is often a wonderfully surprising combination of who and what we *want to* be...*and* who and what we never realized we *could* be.

By exercising our ability to perform, we throw off the shackles of the confined versions of who we are now, these selves based in roles that we and others have given us and that we mistakenly believe narrowly define us. We no longer have to sigh and shake our heads and say we can't do or be something else because "this is just who I am." Because the idea of who we are begins to change when we are reminded to see ourselves and all of those around us as the performers of our lives and of our world. Performance gives us agency and the ability to be change makers. And even though we're always performing, becoming conscious of this ability and finding varied and creative ways to make use of it is what enables us to do all sorts of things before we know how.

Performing Gives Us New Choices

We often say to teams we're working with, "You're going to have your regular meeting, only we're going to do it as a performance."

"Are we doing the meeting or the performance?" is a typical question we get in return.

"We're doing a performance of the meeting."

Carter and Franz, two members of a team from a large ad agency I was coaching, had each been complaining to other staff members about how much they dreaded—and often avoided—their check-in meetings together. Carter, the senior of the two, was a creative director with a self-professed aversion to planning and procedure. He said, "I was seeing these meetings as a kind of bureaucratic exercise that was only tangentially related to my highly pressured, deadline-driven work." Franz, the project manager, always came away from the meetings feeling frustrated and demoralized and lacking the input he needed to move their work along. "I couldn't figure out how to successfully engage Carter in the conversation we needed to have," he said.

And so I directed Carter and Franz to start performing their meetings as a work session on a creative project. I assigned Carter the character of "a skilled creative collaborator" and directed Franz to think of the scene as being primarily about building a great relationship with Carter rather than figuring out the right tactics to complete the planning he came in to do.

After the first meeting, Carter was uncharacteristically enthusiastic. "The most immediate impact of this direction was around time," he said. "Because it was a performance, time was not an element—every moment took the time it needed, and, surprisingly, the meeting didn't last any longer. Franz began by laying out how he saw our task, and when I listened to him as a 'creative collaborator,' I realized I didn't know what he was talking about! And so I asked him questions. His answers were thoughtful, and I started to see him as a professional, with different skills than me, who was working hard—and needed my help—to accomplish something for a larger goal that we both shared. We discovered—right there in the moment—some solutions to issues I had been grappling with. I wasn't just helping him anymore, he was helping me."

Franz (always the quieter of the two) smiled. "Dare I say, the meeting was actually enjoyable. And we got a hell of a lot done."

Indeed, the change is often immediate. By simply stating that the normal activity is going to be a performance, it's no longer "normal." This immediately creates a self-awareness that, in turn, creates the possibility for growth and change. When we perform a meeting, that awareness makes us think twice before we check our phone for the eleventh time, or reconsider how we might state a criticism, or prompts us to participate when we typically might not. Suddenly, we're looking at what's going on not just from our own "normal" point of view but with a new view, from the vantage points of the audience and the other actors. We're thinking like a writer and a director. We can experiment on the spot. We can perform our way out of all sorts of situations that don't work and begin to perform our way into an infinite variety of situations that do.

ACT II

THE BECOMING PRINCIPLE

*The Five Fundamentals
of Performance*

INTRODUCTION TO ACT II

To help you get on the road to enhancing and improving your performances at work, I'm now going to introduce you to what we call the five fundamentals of performance. Each makes up a chapter in Act II.

First I'm going to ask you to *make the choice to grow*. If you do, you'll be amazed at the new possibilities that present themselves.

Then I'm going to show you how to *build ensembles everywhere you go*. As I wrote about in Act I, the kind of growth and development we're working on is not a solitary endeavor.

Next comes a *revolutionary way to have a conversation*, so get ready to stop talking and start listening.

After that, you're going to get *creative in the everyday* as a way to deal with all the crap you get handed (and that you hand out).

And finally, you're going to start *improvising your life* and discover how curveballs become gifts, noes become yeses, and making mistakes can be a cause for celebration.

Curtain up!

Performance Fundamental One:

Choose to Grow

When I let go of what I am, I become what I might be.

—*Lao-tzu*

Braden, a consumer products VP in his forties, was one of twenty-five participants in his company's intensive leadership development program, an experience that was roughly the equivalent of getting an MBA in six months. We were asked to help the program's participants to raise their game as authentic leaders and to grow their emotional intelligence.

We decided there'd be no better way to kick-start our session than with our namesake exercise, the one that inspired us to start the company in 1996. I announced that we were going to give them one minute—sixty whole seconds—to come onstage and give a performance of their lifetime. "You can perform your entire life, or a slice of it," I told them. "You can perform a really big important experience that helped to shape you as a leader, or something small. It can be silly or sad, noisy or quiet. It's up to you. But it *has* to be a performance! Use dialogue, poetry, dance, mime, opera, Kabuki—whatever you want—as long as it's connected to you and your life as a leader."

I could feel a tsunami of fear, anxiety, and dread roll over the group. This was far outside the comfort zone of virtually everyone, let alone the kind of knowers and doers seated uneasily around the room. This exercise is an object lesson in *not knowing* what to do. It's impossible, risky, imposing, unknowable.

Braden felt a particular challenge. "Right away, stuff started racing through my head," he told me later. "What defined me? What changed me? What made me who I am today?"

I explained to the group that we would call people's names, give them a big show-biz introduction, and their colleagues would give them thunderous applause. Then they were going to have a minute for their performance. Then they'd get *more* thunderous applause. (The applause is really important, so I had them practice clapping, stomping, and hooting, which they nailed instantly.) And then they'd stay up in the spotlight while we gave them theatrical direction, inspired by whatever they just did, to perform a "sequel," in which one or more of the POAL team would improvise with them.

As all that began to sink in, we demonstrated a couple of performances of a lifetime of our own, mainly to let them see that this insane thing might just be possible. First, I performed a scene in which I was nervously and neurotically preparing for a meeting I had had a few years back with the former president of Mexico, Vicente Fox, at his hacienda. It was lighthearted and slapstick and made everyone laugh. In the improvised sequel, I was the president of Mexico, in a crisis meeting with my cabinet (played by my fellow POAL trainers), who spoke no English. Then Bradford Jordan, one of our very talented trainers, performed a complex scene in which he was celebrating New Year's Eve on the East Coast at the precise moment that his mother, on the West Coast, was shot and killed in a carjacking. In his sequel, Bradford was joined by another POAL director, who improvised a poem with him called "Letting Go." It was raw and emotional and had a visible impact on everyone, including Braden. "When I saw that second performance and the sequel," he recalled, "I immediately flashed on one of the worst moments of my life. But I knew I did not want to perform *that* in front of my peers."

I then announced that we were going to call ten random people from the audience. The first was a Southern jock who performed a scene about moving from town to town throughout his childhood, having to make friends over and over again each time. In the sequel, he found himself at a party with *all* of those long-lost friends, all reminiscing about "the time we..." A woman from a small town in Iowa performed a vignette about finding a wardrobe full of flamenco costumes in her attic and discovering that her mother had been a successful flamenco artist in a previous lifetime. The sequel? She opened up another closet and found all of the musicians who had performed with her mother, ready to flamenco some more. A tall man with perfect military bearing took us back to his visit at an Air Force base when he was a kid, where he saw an African American man in uniform and it made him hope that someday he, too, could fly. In his sequel, he played his small son, asking his father (himself, played by one of us), what it was like the first time he flew.

Over the course of the one-minute performances, these leaders were showing up in new, surprising, and intimate ways. The sequels were stretching and surprising them even more while making it safe and exciting to do so. They were accessing and unleashing that dormant ability to perform and improvise; their stories about themselves—now breathing new air—were being built upon and created through the sequels and the audience's participation and appreciation.

Meanwhile, even as Braden was enthralled by his colleagues' performances, he was getting increasingly nervous, wondering if he was going to be picked. All he could think about was the story of the darkest moment in his life, one that he had never told even to his closest friends.

Eight of the ten people had been called. A good friend of Braden's was the ninth. She performed a very affecting scene and sequel about saying good-bye to her brother, who died much too early from an aneurysm. As the scene ended, Braden's eyes were filled with tears and he heard his name called. "Even as I walked to the stage," he said, "I kept searching for something else to perform other than the low point of my life. But nothing came to me."

Braden stood in front of the audience. His first line was "I'm sixteen years old." He began acting out a series of moments: a phone call about his failing backpack business...an injury to his rotator cuff...He paced back and forth on the stage, staring at the ground and muttering to himself, revealing fragments of what was clearly making him distraught: having to leave the swim team due to his injury, his parents' divorce, his mother's remarriage, his loneliness and isolation.

Finally, he pulled out a chair and stood up on it. He looked down, trembling. He hesitated for a long moment, and then he jumped. There were gasps in the audience. For a moment he lay still, and then he looked up, shaken, and said: "I'm alive."

The audience of Braden's peers jumped to their feet and cheered. In the sequel, the entire cast of POAL trainers came onstage in two teams, "Death" and "Life," with Braden caught in the middle. They hurled insults at each other, fighting it out until Braden joined the Life team, which carried him to safety. More thunderous applause and people on their feet. A bunch of good friends came and gave Braden hugs. "It was raw," he recalled. "All of my shields were gone."

Beyond Emotional Intelligence

When I talk about the Performance of a Lifetime exercise to people who have not yet experienced it, I get reactions that range from "I want to do that!" to "I would *never* do that!" Sort of like Braden. But after working personally with tens of thousands of people, I can assert that taking that one minute to perform—to break out and momentarily do away with the rules, scripts, personas, and roles that dominate everyday work and life—is a profoundly liberating and rejuvenating human experience. By performing who you are like this, you get a new and unique perspective of yourself. By seeing others perform, you get a new and unique perspective of them. By performing in the sequels, you are immediately initiated into a creative collaboration with others who have been inspired by what you have shared. And as deeply compelling and moving as the beautiful and varied stories that people perform are, what is fundamental to this activity is *that you are doing it* and *that you can*. It's the Becoming Principle in action, and when you take it into the workplace, all the things you, your team, and your company are not (yet) become possible.

Individual and Collective Growing

Braden's performance made a huge impression on everyone that day. In the conversation immediately following the exercise, people commented on how the openness of the performances was contagious, and many spoke of feeling thankful for what one colleague called "being invited in." I noticed one participant had tears running down his face. "I am so grateful for my colleagues' performances," he said. "You think sometimes you are the only one going through hard stuff. I am going through so much right now in my life. It is so helpful to not feel alone."

Growing is not an individual act. It doesn't happen in a vacuum. And you can't do it on your own. Growing is *always* a relational activity. It's dependent on the people you're working, living, interacting, or playing with. So what did *we* all do together that day that made it possible for Braden and everyone else in the room to grow—as colleagues, as people, as leaders? Together we chose to create a new performance, a new kind of conversation, a new way of listening and talking that created an environment for growth. With the support of the group—vigorous applause for each performance, the collective wonderment that everyone experiences at the same time, the heartfelt and immediate appreciation for what each brave soul does, and going somewhere altogether unexpected in the improvised sequels that follow—people are able to do what they normally would not. The Performance of a Lifetime exercise is our signature precisely because it creates an environment in which you can't do what you normally do because, obviously, it's not normal to get up and perform your life in a minute! This environment (which everyone participates in creating) allows the group to choose to grow. Doing what you don't normally do, doing something before you know how with others, that's what growth is and where growth happens.

And you don't need a tight-knit, high-powered group of people like the folks in this program to engender such growth. We've seen it work

"I decided to stop watching and start interacting."

with co-workers who barely spoke to one another, with departments that were cordoned off in silos, and with total strangers. By performing in ways they have never performed together before, they, in turn, create an environment in which everyone, both individually and collectively, grows.

And the growth that people experience isn't limited to the immediate aftermath of the exercise. "When I got back from the program, I came in and talked to my team about how we're going to do things differently," Braden said. "It was an inflection point for our team." Braden told me that one of the more profound areas of growth for him was that he became more genuine in the workplace. "I used to have a tendency to be overly cheerful and smile too much," he said. "I know it came across as insincere. I was saying all the right things, but I wasn't connecting with people. Now, I connect with people a lot more. I talk to people about their personal lives." Braden was recently asking a colleague about his love of fly-fishing. "And now I can say to him, 'I need this package insert to be as elegant as the flies you're tying.' I can say this because I know him on a more personal level."

It wasn't just Braden's work life that was affected. He told me he's become much more comfortable with himself in and out of work. "I appreciate my wife and kids a lot more," he says. "I've been working on new performances there, too. I read my kids more books. We play more basketball in the backyard. My wife and I just came back from the best vacation we've ever had. This experience awakened me and opened me up in a whole new way."

Braden emerged a much more capable, powerful, and inspiring leader. He and the rest of his colleagues used performing their lives in one minute to reactivate performing their work and their lives, period.

Grow Instead of Know

In our contemporary culture, we place a lot of value on being a "knower," having all the answers, and always being right—so much value that saying "I don't know" can seem like the worst thing imaginable. But when we hide what we don't know, or feel bad about it, or are admonished as a result, we miss out on the kind of learning and growth that "not knowing" can produce. And this can be demoralizing and frightening, as another leadership program we did with a group of executives at a consulting firm revealed.

We asked them to come prepared to work on a business relationship they wanted to grow in: to navigate better, expand, and improve how they show up. We asked them to come up with specific situations they were struggling with and turn them into scenes that embodied these challenges.

The first featured six men and a woman named Amy, who had just been transferred from the London office. She was just a few weeks into her new job, which represented a serious leap from her former regional position to one of global and enterprise-wide importance.

In the scene, Amy and her six colleagues performed being on a bus, coming back from a leadership team off-site for the North American organization. The guys were joking around, having a good time, and started talking smack about the (American) football play-offs and the Super Bowl, yukking it up. In the middle of the scrum sat Amy, not saying anything, politely chuckling, clearly having no idea what anyone was talking about.

Finally, she summoned some steadfast British resolve and tried to insert herself into the scene. "So, where are you in the play-offs?" she asked. The guys paused, looked at her, and went right back to talking about who was going to win the Super Bowl, talking trash good-naturedly and carrying on.

I called "Curtain" (that's theater talk for ending the scene) and asked, "Whose scene is this? Who asked for help?" Amy raised her hand. "This is my life right now. I'm new to the North American leadership team, and I'm a Brit. And every meeting looks exactly like this. I can't find my footing on this team!"

I asked the group to weigh in on what they had seen and to give Amy some performance direction for situations like this. People suggested she try to ask questions; to feel comfortable saying, "Whoa, whoa, whoa, guys, you're talking Super Bowl. Teach it to me, I'm new."

Amy said she couldn't say that, no way.

I said, "Okay, fair enough. Let's find out some more about your situation, and see if we can help you to be able to say that, or whatever it turns out you do want to say." I directed her colleagues to learn more about Amy, not to assume anything, and to get closer to her view of the world. So they asked about her background, how she got promoted, how long she'd had the job, what she liked about it, and so on. As Amy talked, it became clear that she had a giant leap to make, not just culturally but in leadership as well. She didn't actually know how to do her job yet. She wasn't even sure precisely what her job was. The group listened intently and acknowledged what a challenging moment she was in.

I could see Amy relaxing amid this support from her colleagues, enough that when I gave her some new lines to say in this scene and directed her to do what her colleagues had suggested (ask questions, push back, and talk a little trash of her own), she went for it. Big-time. She was campy and playful, slapping guys on the back, imitating their body language, teasing them about this "obscure American sport." When we called curtain, people burst into applause. It was like watching an entirely different person. And she was having fun doing it.

Then Amy said, "But I don't think I could ever actually do that."

The room got quiet. I asked her why.

"Look, I'm used to being the one with all the answers. 'Keep calm and carry on' and all that. Now, here I am, I don't know anything and I have to ask people to teach me?"

One of her colleagues spoke up. "Everyone knows that you don't have expertise in the North American market. How could you? That's not why you were promoted! You were promoted because you know how to run a team, a department. You're a leader."

Amy wasn't convinced. "I just want to have something smart to say. I get worried without my expertise. I never realized until this moment how important that is for me, to know what to do and be smart."

"Well, you're clearly smart," I said. "But how about this? What if there is no relationship between being smart and knowing what to do? As your colleagues have said, they wouldn't have moved you across the pond and given you a huge leadership mandate if they didn't see that you're smart and a leader. Seems like now you need to use your smarts to be an enthusiastic learner. That's your performance. That's the leadership performance that your colleagues are giving you to do."

There's no question that Amy *knew* a lot. And in her version of her story, her value and expertise were all due to her knowledge. What she was missing was the huge opportunity for growth that her promotion and relocation provided. It was time for her to "grow instead of know." But before you put that phrase on a bumper sticker, let me explain.

The trap that Amy and so many of us fall into is what Lois Holzman calls the Knowing Paradigm. Simply stated, under the Knowing Paradigm, knowing is everything, and everything can be known. You can't talk about something unless you know about it. You can't do something unless you already know how to do it first. Under the Knowing Paradigm, the only kind of learning that matters is the *acquisitional* kind, where you acquire information, facts, and skills. *Developmental learning* isn't in the picture. Developmental learning involves imagination, play, and growing in the ways that babies do. The reason we put emphasis on developmental learning is this: If you were allowed to do only what you already knew how to do, you would be stuck a babbling baby all your life. You wouldn't learn to talk, walk, dress yourself, do a cartwheel, draw a picture, solve a math problem, or acquire a start-up. You just can't get something "right" until you first get it "wrong."

So developmental learning is actually key for surviving and growing in the constantly changing world we're all navigating, and it can't happen when we're stuck in the Knowing Paradigm. Embracing what you don't know—and the awareness that you don't know it—is part of what's *required* for being a leader in today's world. Leaders lead teams into some future state. The fact that it's the future means inherently that no one can know what is going to happen (if you do in fact have future-knowing capability, call me). You can read every book on the subject, take every class, master every tool at hand, but you can't know everything. This is what Amy came to realize. And she needed the group performance to help her understand this idea and act on it.

What I love about Amy's story is that when you stop and think about it, she was actually playing the role of a true leader from the outset of the exercise. She was the one who told her group that she *did not know* how to deal with being the lone British woman on a team dominated by American men. In her willingness to reveal what she didn't know, she used the group to help solve her problem. Though she asserted that she would never ask for help and admit she didn't know what she was doing, this was *exactly* what Amy did—with terrific results, I might add. Not only did she help herself, but she also opened the eyes of the guys in the scene to the inhospitable environment they had unwittingly created for their co-worker. As they supported her growth, they in turn had to grow.

No One Said It Would Be Easy

While we can enjoy benefits galore when we grow, there's no way of getting around the fact that *growing is hard*. If it were easy (and not important), I wouldn't have written this book.

Jenna is a friend of mine. She's a talented and hardworking national organizer for an environmental organization where she's worked since its founding in 1998. Five years ago, the organization hired a new president, and that's where Jenna's troubles began. Jared, a charismatic fifty-something who'd had a successful career in broadcasting followed by an even more successful run as a new-media maven, was devoting his early retirement and considerable energy to revitalizing the organization. His efforts had paid off, and the organization had grown rapidly. And Jared had shaken the place up. He had a no-nonsense, take-charge style and ran the organization like an Internet start-up. Several of the longtime staffers had butted heads with him early on and resigned, and their replacements were known to the longtimers (privately, of course) as "Jared Juniors."

Jenna was miserable. She and Jared had had a couple of very public spats a few years back, and now they seldom spoke outside of formal settings. She had frequent disputes with the Jared Juniors and often sulked around the office, giving people a hard time. She took everything personally and was angry much of the time. It was difficult for her and no picnic for her friends and close colleagues, either, some of whom were a sort of self-appointed board of performance directors for her. I was one of them, and, frankly, it had been pretty hard for us to help her as much as we'd have liked. Whether due to her passionate dedication to the cause or sheer stubbornness, Jenna had stayed in her job and had mostly rejected our repeated attempts to help her get better at navigating her workplace. At a time when she could have felt the most proud of all the work she and her colleagues had put in over the years, she felt isolated and unmotivated.

But not untalkative. We were all having dinner together one night and Jenna was holding forth. It seemed she had been left off a meeting invite that day and caused a bit of a scene in the office as a result. With us, she was ranting about how it wasn't an accident, how she was being sidelined, excluded, underappreciated, and disrespected, and how it was all because of "that jerk Jared and his mini-me's."

I looked around at the others at the table. Patricia appeared to be studying the napkin in her lap. Kishanda, who works in Jenna's office and witnessed her performance that day, met my glance and gave me a knowing look. Jenna was obviously very upset, but we had heard it all so many times before, we were getting a bit frustrated.

Kishanda cleared her throat loudly to get Jenna's attention. After three tries, it worked. "So, Jenna," she said. "Would you like to finally do something about this?"

"Uh, duh, yeah. That would be good. Wanna sign a petition on my behalf?"

Kishanda put down her fork. "No, girl, I don't. I'm not wasting good ink on getting you into some meeting you think you should be in. You need to take a look and listen to what you sound like."

Jenna looked surprised, then angry. She growled: "What do you mean? What do I sound like?"

I said, "A pain in the butt."

Patricia said, "Sort of childish."

Kishanda said, "And you're high-maintenance."

Jenna immediately got defensive (really, who wouldn't?) and started to protest. "Whoa, what? Why am I the pain in the butt? What do you mean, high-maintenance? If you were in my shoes, you'd feel the exact same way!"

I jumped on the bandwagon. "You're really being impossible, Jenna. Why can't you hear what we're saying? This has been going on forever."

Kishanda leaned forward and clasped Jenna's hands. "Honey, I actually do know the situation, and no, I wouldn't feel the same way. I know things are not perfect at our organization; how could they be? Everyone has their shit. But you're not the victim here. We have to work with you. *Every day.* We know you feel this way. And it's exhausting. That's what it means to be high-maintenance!"

Jenna shook her head, and we could see her holding back tears.

Kishanda said softly, "Jenna, do you think that anything we're saying is...at least...*possible*?"

Jenna was silent. For at least a minute. Finally she asked, "What do you mean?"

Patricia looked up. "Does any of this even sound familiar to you?"

Another silence, a little shorter. "Yeah...I mean, it's not totally *unfa-miliar* to me," she said. "But—"

Kishanda cut her off. "Okay. Good. Let's go with 'not unfamiliar.' You don't have to agree with all of it. Not unfamiliar is fine."

Patricia and I nodded in support. Kishanda continued. "So what if you were to *try it on* for a while?"

Jenna looked at us quizzically. "Try it on? Try what on?"

Kishanda was ready. "That you can be difficult. High-maintenance. Try on that you can be that way. Like a suit that's a completely different style from what you usually wear. Try it on."

Jenna looked down at her almost untouched Cobb salad, then at each of us in turn. Nobody blinked. She sighed—loudly.

"Okay. I'll try"—and she gave a small, mischievous smile—"it on."

So, what's with this "trying it on"? Kishanda showed me something that night that I hadn't seen before (and writing this book has given me a chance to explore further): *Trying it on* is a particularly useful performance direction. It allows you to act and think in a new and different way, without necessarily "agreeing" with it. Herminia Ibarra, author of *Act Like a Leader, Think Like a Leader* and a professor of organizational behavior at INSEAD, calls this "committed flirtation" and points to the benefits of embracing new possibilities *as if* they were realistic and desirable, but without "committing" to them as anything more than playful experiments.

Trying it on gets you out of the "knowing" space (*I know exactly what's going on here and you don't*) and into a more curious and wondering space (*Hmm. If this is true, what else might be going on?*). It makes choosing to grow, even in the face of extremely difficult circumstances, a little easier.

And that's a good thing, as Jenna was about to discover. Because sometimes growth isn't just about developing new performances you haven't tried before but also about coming face-to-face with the (often pretty awful, difficult, ineffective, you fill in the blank) performances you've been doing for a long, long time. Fred Newman called this "radical acceptance." Radical acceptance allows us to look in the mirror and embrace who we are now (even as we're looking ahead to who we're becoming). And, boy, we don't always like what we see. Trying it on allows us to hold up that mirror but take a sidelong glance. Sometimes that can help.

For Jenna, this sidelong glance connected her to her colleagues in a new and different way because it let her see herself as they saw her and "radically accept" that view. She was able to consider the strong words we threw at her without getting angry or fleeing (her two usual performance choices when she felt challenged). By trying it on—flirting with it, but not necessarily marrying it yet—Jenna was able to hear and do something different and re-enter her workplace in a nondefensive way.

"Just today," Jenna told me, "we were in a meeting where Jared and I disagreed on something, again. Of course everybody else took his side. Well, you know what I would normally do. But instead, I paused...I just shut up for a minute and listened to where everybody was coming from. And I hate to admit it, but I definitely heard things about their point of view that I had totally missed. So I'm calling that pause my 'trying it on' performance. It let me move on and actually be present for what was being discussed." She smiled. "Thanks for kicking my butt."

Radical acceptance requires bravery. And the growth that springs from it requires bravery as well. Growth is unpredictable and sometimes treacherous. You don't know how to do what you're doing, so you're going to make mistakes and take wrong turns. But deep and lasting transformation can occur when our belief systems and the often undermining stories that we hold on to are challenged, reconsidered, and refreshed. This is not to say we will suddenly feel no pain or insecurity, or become brand-new people. But part of how the Becoming Principle works is that we can question the assumption that things are just the way they are, and that we are nothing more than who we are or have been.

Switching It Up

Most of us have been trained to lead with our strengths. And most leaders and managers want to assign roles according to the perceived strengths and weaknesses of the individuals on their teams. This is natural and makes sense. But often it's not growth-friendly. The legendary dancer and choreographer Twyla Tharp said, "If you only do what you know and do it very, very well, chances are that you won't fail. You'll just stagnate, and your work will get less and less interesting, and that's failure by erosion."

What does that look like in everyday work?

"Suresh should introduce the presentation because he has a commanding voice."

"Julie should do the spreadsheets because she's so detail-oriented."

"I'm a terrible writer, so I'll hand the copy off to Jeff."

We can get stuck in roles like this and never develop new ones, not because we can't, but because we don't put ourselves in situations where we can perform differently and that allow us to grow beyond what we know. When we work with an organization to grow its people, we almost always divide the participants into smaller groups to do scene work. And when they divvy up the roles, we see a consistent pattern: The outgoing person will be the one to take on the most dramatic part of the scene. The shy person will mime something in the background. The funny person will crack the jokes. You get the idea. So as we go from group to group, we ask if they're here to solve a problem or to learn and grow. Of course, the answer is the latter. So if that's the goal, why would you want to do the things you're already good at? Hmm.

The truth is, these roles aren't as fixed as we think they are anyway. Might the outgoing person be able to successfully mime in the background? Might the shy person have a sly sense of humor? Might the funny lady create drama? The answer to these questions is almost always yes. But the only way we'll ever find out is by performing. That's why, if you really want to grow, my first instruction to you is to play some new roles. Switch it up. And start looking for opportunities for your people to take on roles they never would have imagined taking on.

Choosing to grow is a constant back-and-forth between doing the things you're good at and doing the things you're not good at. I'm not saying to throw out what you're good at. I'm saying to find new strengths by exploring undeveloped muscles or weaknesses. By consciously choosing how you want to act, you inherently make the choice to grow.

How exactly does this growth happen? And what will the results of it be? We don't know. That's what makes growing so scary and so exciting at the same time. But one thing is certain—you don't have to go it alone. In fact, you can't. For Braden, Amy, and Jenna, the groups they were a part of (or as I prefer to call them, *ensembles*) had everything to do with making their growth possible. And that's what our next fundamental is all about.

Choose to Grow Exercises

1. Challenge the Knowing Paradigm by spending at least a day at work performing "not knowing." Make the choice to be uncertain, tolerant of ambiguity, and open, rather than having or even searching for an answer or explanation. Say things like, "I have no idea!," or "Let's sit with this for a while," or "There might not be a clear answer here."

2. Practice radical acceptance by thinking about something that a friend or colleague has brought up with you, or about you, that was difficult to hear and that you have rejected. Try it on for a while. Consider it as a possibility. See what you learn about yourself and what new performances you can create as a result.

3. Put yourself in a situation in which you have to do something that might make you say, "I couldn't possibly do that"—something you don't know how to do or you're not good at. Take a stab at a stretch assignment (e.g., volunteer for a project you wouldn't normally take on). Have a different kind of conversation than you typically have (e.g., give someone difficult feedback, ask for feedback, state a disagreement, or agree for a change).

Performance Fundamental Two:

Build Ensembles Everywhere

A human being is a part of the whole called by us "Universe"... He experiences himself, his thoughts and feelings as something separated from the rest— a kind of optical delusion of his consciousness.

—*Albert Einstein*

One day in January, I got on the A train at Thirty-Fourth Street in Manhattan for a thirty-minute ride out to Brooklyn. My earbuds were in, and I was listening to Alabama Shakes, paying no attention to my fellow subway riders. After a couple of stops, I noticed some people across the car were starting to giggle and shyly point at something. I looked up. A businessman in an expensive-looking camel coat was taking his pants off. Two young women in their twenties—one, seated, with blue hair and lots of studs in her ears, and another standing with a short natural 'fro and sunglasses—took off their skirts. A middle-aged man dressed in all black except for his white tallis fringes and a big fur hat let his pants fall. I noticed, thankfully, that they were all wearing underwear. A few stops more, and a number of other people came on. Bundled up in down coats, a mom, dad, and two-year-old came into view... and none were wearing pants. I knew I wasn't hallucinating because it looked like everyone else on the subway was seeing the same thing I was seeing.

The subway car had been filled with a bunch of isolated individuals who previously avoided eye contact with others at all costs but who were now in the same scene, having a shared experience as a group. We were laughing. We were pointing. We were making faces at one another. We were taking pictures. We were jabbing one another with an elbow.

I suppose I should explain. Improv Everywhere, a performance art group started by the very clever Charlie Todd, goes around "causing scenes," as they call it. They do these performance pranks in public places, including the annual "No Pants Subway Ride." Since 2002, on a designated day, tens of thousands of people in more than sixty countries get on trains without their pants on.

When the pants-less people left the car, there was a completely different feeling among the riders. My fellow subway car passengers and I were seemingly transformed from atomized individuals into a socially connected group, all in the blink of a disbelieving eye. We were not alone! And all it took was a bunch of strangers taking off their pants.

But you know what? On the A train that day, what was uncovered was the togetherness that was there all the time. While most Western cultures herald individuality as *the* essential human characteristic, humans are a social species. And we don't need an A train full of Fruit of the Looms and Victoria's Secrets to be a group. We're already in them—from our families to our various teams and relationships at work, from the folks in the elevator you just rode up in to the crowd at the food truck all vying for burritos. We live our lives and do our work with others, in groups.

But there is a paradox here. While we are *part of* groups all the time, that's far from the whole story. Groups, or teams—or, in the theatrical language we use at POAL, *ensembles*—don't just exist. They have to be actively created. They have to be *built*. Otherwise, we can fall sway to the culture that makes us think we're just atomized individuals. This second fundamental of the Becoming Principle is all about the enormous value and the creative process of seeing—*and building*—ensembles, everywhere.

What's So Great About Ensembles?

As an actor, improviser, and singer, I have been part of performing ensembles all my life and have experienced their power firsthand. Acting in a play, playing with a band, or performing improv comedy are intensive ensemble experiences. Working and playing with a range of talents, inputs, styles, disciplines, materials, and ideas is stimulating, creative, exhausting, invigorating, humbling, developmental, and fun. When it works well, you're creating art, which builds the ensemble, which creates more art, which further builds the ensemble, and on and on.

In their book, *Yes, And*, authors Kelly Leonard and Tom Yorton of the

Second City make a most interesting point about teams versus ensembles. They note that teams are often gathered together to compete, to fight an external foe (think sports teams). But ensembles, they say, carry no such baggage. An ensemble is "a thing unto itself, an entity that is only its true self when its members are performing as one." I'd like to add that an ensemble is something entirely different from the individuals who make it up. It's apples and oranges instead of more apples or more oranges. What makes an ensemble unique is that it acts, works, and speaks in many voices; has lots of eyes and ears; has its own personalities and sensibilities; can turn left and right, stand and sit simultaneously; can leave the room and still be there; can agree and disagree at the same time.

Our old pal Lev Vygotsky has helped me appreciate the awesomeness of building ensembles. He studied how children learn and develop, including, as we've discussed, the value of supporting them in "performing a head taller" (essentially doing what they don't know how to do as a key part of their developmental learning). One of the places where performing a head taller happens is what Vygotsky called the "Zone of Proximal Development," or ZPD, in which skilled people interact and learn alongside less skilled people.

Back in the mid-1990s, I worked with the Barbara Taylor School, an experimental elementary school in New York City that was using Vygotsky's principles. Instead of forming classes strictly divided by age, we organized the students into groups of multiple ages. Together, with the assistance of an adult teacher/director, these little ensembles played, performed, and discussed their subject matter, from algebra to zoology. As Vygotsky predicted, the little ones, surrounded by their more skilled ensemble-mates, performed a head taller and learned at an impressive rate. And the older students—actively engaged in the joint and creative activity of learning/teaching/performing—learned how to teach and collaborate, which deepened and expanded their grasp of the material. The result was that the *entire* class learned. The Barbara Taylor School was short-lived, but its impact on me has been lifelong. The learning and growth of those groups of children occurred not *despite* their differences but *because* of them.

Over the years, as I've continued to observe, build, and work with groups in all walks of life and occupations, I've come to see and appreciate

"We should all hang out together sometime."

that the most creative and productive ensembles are made up of people with different skills, different experiences, different temperaments, and varied points of view. It's the diversity of the group that provides the material for new ideas, new ways to talk and work together. Building diverse ensembles makes it possible for everyone to give something and for everyone to learn. If you build with the rich material that a diverse group brings together, the ensemble is able to accomplish much more, and with greater creativity and collective wisdom. We *all* get to perform a head taller.

Ensembles Are Good for Our Health

An academic medical center asked us to come in to help with a crucial scene in the delivery of patient care: the performance of nurses when patients from emergency medicine are transferred to general medicine. It's known as the "handoff," and all sorts of things can—and do—go wrong if the two departments aren't working well together.

When we first met the personnel in the emergency medicine and general medicine departments, the tension was so high that nurses from one side were arguing, screaming, and even hanging up the phone on nurses from the other side as they negotiated the numerous handoffs that happened every single day. Nurses from each side were regularly going to their managers with an endless litany of complaints: *Emergency didn't*

complete the patient chart correctly... Medicine doesn't get that we're over-
loaded and are dealing with knife wounds, near fatal loss of blood... Emer-
gency keeps sending us patients covered in shit and we have to spend time
cleaning them up instead of attending to their medical care... I have to talk
to three different nurses to hand over information on a patient... Beds can't
be ready when they send us patients at a shift change... And on top of the
specifics, the nurses were highly stressed by the streams of paperwork
and documentation, not to mention the emotional wear and tear of dealing with trauma, illness, and death.

None of this stress was new, but it was a *big* problem. Seventy percent
of the patients in the general medicine wards came from emergency medicine. The hospital had tried all sorts of interventions over the years, but
according to Claudine, the director of nursing, "Nothing had worked. I
knew I needed to bring something in that would knock people's socks
off, get them out of their comfort zone, and where the end result would
be greater collaboration and ultimately better care of our patients."

As we talked with Claudine, it became clear that emergency and
general medicine were in a bad, but not unusual, play. They were like
the individuals with their earbuds in on my subway ride to Brooklyn:
an ensemble waiting to be created, but in the meantime feeling discon-
nected and alienated. The thing was, this ensemble *needed* to be created,
because the outcome of the scenes in this play could mean life or death.

When we brought the leadership of both departments together for an
all-day session, there was a palpable "us versus them" atmosphere in the
room, and—aside from some glaring—little contact between the two
groups. Some of the nurses knew one another from talking on the phone;
a few had worked together in another unit. But most of them were somewhere between strangers and estranged.

We started our work together with a theatrical warm-up, and as weird
as some of the other exercises I've shown you are, this one takes the
cake. Naturally, it's one of my favorites. We gathered all sixty nurses in
a large circle and directed them to begin moving at an excruciatingly
slow pace. This was both physically and mentally difficult to do, especially for these nurses, who spend most days saving lives by moving as
fast as they possibly can. But soon they appeared to be defying gravity,
and in their blue and green and daisy-covered scrubs, they looked like
an idiosyncratically costumed modern dance troupe. In order to follow

our increasingly bizarre directions—to make eye contact, make a funny face, and then talk with one another about their day in gibberish—they began to take cues from one another. As they stifled their laughter and embarrassment as best they could, I could see that an ensemble was, albeit slowly, making its entrance onto the stage.

Then we conducted our signature One-Minute Performance of a Life-time exercise. The nurses performed scenes of their lives that would have both broken your heart and caused severe abdominal pain from laughter (you would have been okay, though—lots of really good nurses around). They were crying and laughing together, having fun with people with whom they had never even been civil.

"It's hard to be nasty when you're having fun," Claudine said later. "I was actually watching them build relationships through their laughter and their tears." The nurses were creating this new ensemble through performing, improvising, and taking risks together.

Then came a potentially explosive exercise. We put them in six groups of ten, each comprising a mix of emergency and general medicine nurses. We gave them their performance assignment: "Half of the groups are going to solve all of emergency's problems. The other half are going to solve all of medicine's problems."

I got a lot of skeptical looks. An emergency nurse asked, "What if the medicine nurses don't understand our side of the story?" Heads nodded and I heard murmurs of agreement.

"Well, what if the emergency folks don't get where *we're* coming from?" More nods and crossed arms.

"Great questions," I said. "You'll perform and pretend that you do. Pretend that this is what your job is. Anything you still don't understand, you'll ask one of your ensemble members to teach you. The only rules are that you have to solve the assigned department's woes, and that's it. You've got ninety minutes for this performance. Go!"

And go they did. We walked around periodically to offer directorial help and to make sure that no one was surreptitiously complaining about something from "their" department. But nobody was. These nurses from opposite sides of the hospital fence were performing as if they were on the *same* side and part of the *same* ensemble. Which, of course, they were.

When we came back together to hear them report on their recommen-dations, it was something to behold. They shared an array of solutions.

Some would be easy to implement because the people in the room were empowered to do so right away. Some were more difficult because they were systemic and would involve buy-in from the higher-ups. Everyone thought virtually every idea was a good one. The nurses listened with amazement and a little bit of pride to their new ensemble performing music to everyone's ears.

As striking and important as the results of the session were, what mattered to Claudine was the process and longer-term outcome. She needed not just for these nurses to get along for one day but for both siloed departments to perform as an ensemble going forward, which was precisely the result of these exercises. Immediately, they were able to implement some of the new protocols they had come up with together, and the nurses' openness and ability to talk to one another continued. The phone hang-ups stopped. In surveys six months after this program, the overwhelming majority of emergency medicine and general medicine nurses reported a marked improvement in relationships and processes as a result of the ensemble-building session.

"When you push people outside their comfort zone and they live through it," Claudine said, "it's like when you go through a traumatic experience together. You suddenly see the same people differently. And without that environment, you can have every protocol under the sun and get nowhere."

The Magical Properties of Ensembles

There's a reason companies spend so much money trying to get their teams to work well together. They make the effort because they know that teams that work well together are more creative, productive, and innovative. This not only produces great work, it produces happier employees who are adding value and who feel appreciated and respected. Research shows that investing in creating a culture of collaboration is key to retaining talent. On the positive side, employees from ninety-six of *Fortune*'s "100 Best Companies to Work For" in 2015 cited teams or teamwork among their top reasons for why their companies stood out as great places to work. And on the negative side, a Gallup organization meta-analysis of more than ten thousand businesses found that among the top five reasons people quit their jobs, two involved a lack of teamwork and cooperation. Bottom line: Healthy ensembles = happy employees. But *how* do you build them?

We're told: "There is no 'I' in team"..."A chain is only as strong as its weakest link"..."The whole is greater than the sum of its parts." I've always liked those sayings, but they don't tell you how to get rid of the "I," strengthen the chain, or find the whole. Ensembles or teams don't just pop into existence and get to work (or play). They are created by their members and leaders, together. Mediation consultants and authors Stephen Littlejohn and Kathy Domenici write, "People support what they create." So the challenge—and it's an exciting one—is how to support people in creating their ensembles so they, in turn, can support what they've created.

Several years ago we were working with the United States Olympic team as they prepared for the Summer Games in Beijing. We were working with the American athletes to help build Team USA and to support them in their varied performances off the field of play—dealing with the media, supporting one another within their own teams, navigating family pressures, handling the scene in the Olympic Village, and more. We worked with an average of 125 athletes at a time, including two gold medal–winning men's team shooters, several first-time sprinters, the men's water polo team, and the gold medal–winning women's beach volleyball team. It was quite a diverse group and about as competitive as they come.

We played a game with them that highlights some of the magical properties of ensembles. It went like this: The group spread out across a ballroom-sized space. Each person was asked to single out two other people in the group without letting them know that they were being chosen. Then we asked each person to create an equilateral triangle with those other two people, in silence, again without the others knowing that they were the ones who were supposed to be in that triangle.

It was chaos for the first three minutes. Each person—even the consummate team players—focused single-mindedly on trying to make his or her own triangle work, creating mayhem, and very few triangles, in the process. (Sound familiar?) We let this go on until it was clear they were not getting anywhere. We then blew a whistle and shouted, "Freeze!" Everyone was frustrated, amused, or both.

Then we made one small change. We gave a simple performance

direction: Take responsibility for the entire group to succeed. "Create your triangle at the same time that you make sure we're creating triangles everywhere," we told them. "See the total ensemble, the entire organization as it were, and make it work for everyone."

And then, something utterly magical happened. Armed with the simple idea that they were now working on the entire ensemble succeeding, in a couple of minutes flat, *everyone* was in their equilateral triangles. When the athletes reached this point, they looked around in a collective *Whaaa?*, trying to figure out how this was possible. Why and how could taking responsibility for the whole ensemble make what had been impossible a few seconds before into a success? Why would simply giving the performance direction, "Now work as an ensemble," alter the outcome?

It's as if we'd changed the camera shot in a movie. They had been looking at a tightly framed close-up that showed only three people in motion. But now, it was like the moment in an old Busby Berkeley musical when the camera from above revealed that a group of dancers was actually a human kaleidoscope that we otherwise never would have seen. They could see the big picture, an ensemble performance that was a whole different activity. And not only could they see it, we had invited them to be a creator, a builder of that ensemble.

The supercompetitive Olympians went from *I, alone, have a challenge to meet,* to *I have to build an ensemble to meet the challenge.* By giving each person the responsibility to build this ensemble, a new entity was born, and it began to take responsibility for itself. It still feels like magic every time it happens, but that simple shift in focus and action makes the impossible possible.

Here's another, perhaps unexpected attribute of ensembles that work well together: When we participate in building one, we actually have an opportunity to get to know ourselves in ways we haven't before. I know that a lot of conventional psychological wisdom (and a lot of time on couches) is devoted to the search for "who *I* am." But after years of building and helping others build ensembles of a multitude of shapes, sizes, and purposes, I have seen over and over again that if you want to find out who you are, the groups you're in are a great place to start.

In *The Book: On the Taboo Against Knowing Who You Are*, the philosopher Alan W. Watts wrote, "Other people teach us who we are. Their attitudes to us are the mirror in which we learn to see ourselves... We are, perhaps, rather dimly aware of the immense power of our social environment." I'll put it another way: We often can't see ourselves because we *are* ourselves. But when we're a part of creating something bigger than ourselves, when we are performing as an ensemble together, we are no longer focused simply on ourselves. Everything we do—our words, our gestures, our participation—is received and responded to by others, and that social environment lets us know who we are.

Leading Ensembles into Existence

Sometimes leaders get to choose their teams, but more often they inherit them. Whatever the circumstances, there's a fundamental step they can't afford to skip: They have to craft a performance that will support the creation, development, and growth of a high-performing team—or in our language, a kick-ass ensemble.

After twenty years at a large pharmaceutical company as a senior vice president in technology, Jackson joined a competing company, reporting to the chief information officer. They were going through a company-wide technology transformation, and Jackson's job was to lead it. It was a huge challenge, as was the team he was given to lead. "Most of my direct reports have been there for years," he explained. "And there is a lot of resistance to the technology overhaul I was brought in to design and implement."

Jackson's team had also been leaderless for some time and, as a result, was fractured. Everyone was running what was essentially his or her own private franchise, so they didn't actually think of themselves as a team at all. Jackson had to get the leaders of these franchises to reimagine, redesign, and in some cases relinquish their individual goals in favor of accomplishing the company's goal. Not surprisingly, they were wary about this. Especially since the new guy at the helm had some baggage of his own.

While this would be a hard task for anyone, Jackson had a particular (and in my experience, not that unusual) challenge that wasn't helping the situation. Though he was funny and had a geeky charm, Jackson was also a really smart guy with a brain that could handle more details and data than I even know how to describe. That's why he got the job in the first place—he had the technical knowledge, the expertise, and the experience to make this transformation happen. The problem was that Jackson not only *was* the smartest guy in the room, he also saw himself as and *acted like* the smartest guy in the room. He talked for looooong stretches. In one-on-one meetings, in town halls, in the elevator—he weighed everyone down with an unending stream of technical data, delivered in the professorial tones of a dedicated know-it-all.

As part of getting our work together off the ground, I observed the first day of an off-site Jackson was running with his team in Vancouver. The group was having a lively discussion, with two leaders in the front of the room capturing key points on flip charts, just about everyone in the room participating, everyone engaged, and laughter here and there.

Jackson, sitting in the center of room, was performing in an entirely different scene. His arms were folded, his brow was furrowed, and when there was a pause in the discussion, he launched: "Here's what you're all missing," he said dismissively. "It's most important to recognize blah blah blah. If you are too focused on a, b, c versus d, e, f, and g, you will never get to x, y, z." (Trust me, you don't need the details.)

Kablam! The discussion came to a screeching halt. And it was down-hill from there. Jackson began his professor performance, explaining in detail what people "needed to understand." The leaders up front sat down, people began to look out the windows at the beautiful snow-capped mountains, and some gazed at the floor or their phones.

It was going to be a long three days.

We talked that day on a walk after lunch, and he shared his frustration. He wanted much, much more from his team than they were currently giving, but he was asking people who hardly knew him—who were downright suspicious of him—to take a giant leap of faith. "I know I've got stuff I need to change in my leadership style," he said, "but they just don't get it. They want to take baby steps instead of making a trans-formational leap."

I asked Jackson what he observed about his own performance that morning. He thought for a minute. "I don't know," he said. "I thought I was doing okay, but they got pretty checked out after a while, and I couldn't get them back."

"How about before that?" I asked. "Before you started speaking, there was lots of energy. They were giving one another and you a lot."

"They were?" He was incredulous.

"Yup. It just wasn't what you wanted."

Jackson stopped walking. I did, too.

"And you *told* them that," I said. "Not in so many words, but your performance said, 'What you're saying sucks, you're idiots, and I'm a lot smarter than you.'"

"Ouch. That's exactly what I was thinking," Jackson said.

"I could tell. And so could they."

"Oh, crap," he said. "If I'm alienating them like that, we're in trouble."

"Exactly. Your job is to do this *with* the team, by building with what they give you."

He made a face. "Even if what they're giving is idiotic?"

"Especially if you think it's idiotic," I said. "That's the crap, the chaos, the diversity, and the mix of what you can create with. That's what it means to build and be part of an ensemble."

This is where Vygotsky and the Zone of Proximal Development (ZPD) really get a workout. By creating *with*, not despite, everyone's various inputs and differences, it's possible to build an ensemble that makes everyone smarter and more effective. And that includes all of us dimwits, problem children, and smarty-pants.

"Arrggh," Jackson said. "I don't know how to do that. As you saw this morning."

"Yup," I said. "The great thing about performance is that you get to do a take two."

We brought Jackson's team back together after lunch, and we started the afternoon session off by leading them in "Clap-Pass," a warm-up exercise where you have to synchronize with the group as you pass a rhythmic clap to others around the circle. The ten minutes the group spent figuring out how to do this together was priceless. These self-described tech geeks didn't have much rhythm at all, so the playing field was leveled and fun began to make its way back into the room.

Next on the agenda was a panel with three of the team's leaders. The panel got under way, and within five minutes I could see Jackson beginning to do the arm-folding, head-shaking, and scowling performance. Everyone in the room could see it, too, including the panelists, and you could feel the energy start to fade. I caught Jackson's eye and imitated the same scowling face and body movements that he was making. He froze in an "oh, no!" moment (gotta love this guy). And then he mouthed the words *take two* to me. I nodded.

Jackson sat up, repositioned his seat, and started to perform looking interested. He nodded on occasion, and I saw him taking a few notes. When the presentations finished he led the room in applause, which I could see surprised everybody. They clapped along, carefully, waiting for what was going to happen next. Jackson stood up and thanked everyone for their work. And then he faced the panel and said, "This is great. Thank you again. I want to build on all the work that you've done so far, and I'm thinking about what would be best to do now. What would you guys find most helpful to support you in continuing to move forward with your work? Would you like us to ask questions, challenge you, look for the holes? Are there questions that you have for us? Can we be of help in any way?"

I saw the presenters light up. Then I saw the audience—you know, the ensemble—lean forward. There was a moment of silence, and then a panelist said, "Well, that would be great. We'd love some feedback on what we're describing. We need to know how this links with what you're working on, or doesn't. And yes, what are any holes you see that might reflect our not seeing the broader picture?"

The conversation took off from there, with Jackson soliciting comments from the whole group, including from some folks who hardly ever spoke. He asked people who weren't usually at the front of the room to write on the whiteboard, added on to questions that people raised, and asked more questions that kept the conversation robust and spirited. Jackson even deferred to others on a few occasions. Our leader was getting a feel for leading by building the ensemble, and, by golly, we had ourselves a genuine ZPD.

We took another walk that evening and talked about the day. Jackson could barely contain his excitement. "I hadn't seen how much I had been trying to control...everything," he said. "Being focused on building the ensemble, I had to give up a bit of control. And after a while, I actually *wanted* to give up control, because I was hearing the team say stuff that frankly I had never heard before. And that inspired me and gave me a chance to provide input on things that hadn't surfaced yet."

Six months later, the team had aligned around the new technology strategy and was beginning to partner around execution. I was observing their year-end leadership meeting, and a few minutes before it started, Jackson brought me up to date. "At the last few leadership team meetings everyone was less judgmental and argumentative with one another," he said. "They clearly had been getting that performance from me in the first place. People who report to me are saying they've got more voice. They feel more heard. I'm getting positive reinforcement for these changes."

A few minutes into the meeting, a heated disagreement broke out about how to handle some pushback they'd been getting from their internal business partners. As I observed the team's process, I saw most people advocating for their positions and not doing much listening—pretty typical for any team. But what happened next wasn't typical. Bob, an eighteen-year veteran of the company, spoke up. "Look at us, guys," he said. "I'm not sure this is the kind of conversation we need to be having. We're all blowing our own horns. How about we take a break and start fresh when we come back?"

There was silence for a moment. I looked at Jackson, and he mimed the lip-zipping gesture and smiled. Around the room, I got the sense that people were taking a mental step back to get a better look at their ensemble. A few actually smiled. And Jackson said, "Excellent idea, Bob. Let's do a take two."

Ensemble USA

By the way, here's how the US team did that year in Beijing: The United States won a total of 110 medals, its best count ever in nonboycotted Games. They won more silver and bronze medals than any other participating nation. And I was very interested to learn that US *team-based* sports had been especially successful. Men's and women's basketball won gold, as did men's volleyball, men's and women's beach volleyball, women's soccer, women's eight in rowing, and the men's and women's 4x400-meter relay. In addition, women's volleyball, softball, and baseball; both men's and women's team all-around gymnastics; men's fencing sabre team; women's fencing foil and sabre teams; and both men's and women's water polo won silver and bronze medals. So Team—and ensemble—USA kicked butt. It would be *ridiculous* for POAL to take any credit for this. But, hey. Just saying.

For Jackson, the nurses, and the Olympians, building an ensemble made all the difference. And for any ensemble to get work done, the people who make it up have to be able to talk to one another. Easy, right? Not in my experience—mainly because conversations require *listening*, and that's something most of us are just not very good at. Our next fundamental is all about how.

Build Ensembles Everywhere Exercises

1. Create a ZPD. Bring people together to work on a project who have varied skills, are at different levels, and are different from one another in other ways. Talk about these differences and about your strengths and weaknesses, and work on your project, enthusiastically making use of all of it. Not clear what I mean? Not a problem. Figuring out how to do that together (i.e., deciding together what that means) is part of the ensemble-building process.

2. Spend a week using "we" every time you would normally say "I."

3. Put aside some time in a meeting, or with a friend, family member, or team, and ask the questions "How are we doing this together? Could we do this better? How do we think we're working and communicating together as a ____ (project team, department, marriage [!])." Don't rush to solve a problem or come up with a solution. Be focused on having the conversation—as an ensemble.

4. Be a casting director. Prepare for a meeting by thinking through what roles everyone might be able to play. Don't reserve this for "special occasions," such as project kickoffs or other new endeavors (but don't leave them out, either). Have a conversation together discussing who's doing what when and where, and how the ensemble wants to work together.

create understand empathize look hear accept focus concentr
sent hear offers co-create be quiet surprise embrace build toge
hize look hear accept focus concentrate be present hear offers
ogether ask collabo...   engage learn create under
hize look hear a...   he present empathize
ntrate be pres...   together ask collab
stand empat...   ntrate be present
understan   concentrate be cu
e present   embrace build
er empat   be present hea
ogether   create under
hize lool   hear offers a
ntrate be   r ask collab
stand en   be present
underst   centrate buil
create un   concentrate
sent hear   build toge
hize look   ear offers
ogether as   under
hize look h   offers
ntrate be pre   ask collab
stand empath   e present
and empathize   present a
understand em   ntrate be c
e present hear of   nbrace build
er empathize lool   present hea
ogether ask colla   reate unders
ear accept focus   ers empathize
ntrate be present   d together ask collab
stand empathize   ncentrate be present
understand emp   focus understand buil
create understan   ccept focus concentrate
sent hear offers   ask collaborate hear o
stand empath   build together be presen
understan   t focus concentrate buil
n create   ar accept focus concentr
hize loo   be present accept empa
under   focus concentrate be cu
e pres   rprise embrace build

5

Performance Fundamental Three:

Listen!: The Revolutionary Way to Have a Conversation

I need to listen well so that I hear what is not said.
—*Thuli Madonsela*

It was Sara's idea to bring in the interns. A marketing manager at a global luxury clothing brand, Sara had seen the young people the summer before in a neighboring department—at the copy machine, running up to the front desk to get a FedEx out on time, and in the snack area. She had asked her supervisor about whether her department could do the same this year. She was looking to make a difference in the world and to be a mentor to someone. Her supervisor had agreed and Sara was thrilled.

A word about these interns: They're part of a program called the Development School for Youth (DSY), sponsored by the All Stars Project, a national nonprofit that works to transform the lives of young people from poor, inner-city communities using the developmental power of performance in partnership with caring adults. My business partners and I are some of those caring adults—we're active as longtime volunteers and supporters, and bringing the performance approach to the poorest communities in our country has always been an important part of POAL's social mission.

The DSY works with hundreds of inner-city teenagers every year who participate in workshops, classes, tours, and conversations with business, cultural, and government leaders, and they "perform a head taller" by learning about and performing as professionals such as Wall Street executives, advertising agency creatives, and museum curators. Then these young people are placed in paid, six-week summer internships in Fortune 1000 businesses that partner with the All Stars. For most of them, it's their first paid job other than babysitting or flipping burgers. Or at all.

For Sara and several hundred others each summer, being a DSY intern supervisor entails a performance that introduces the young people to the world of work, including getting to their jobs on time, dressing the part, handling responsibility, looking people in the eye, and dealing with boredom (some of them get better at this than a lot of businesspeople I know). They're encouraged to treat the interns as young employees who want to learn, grow, contribute to, and be part of a broader, mainstream world. And each spring POAL trains hundreds of supervisors from more than one hundred major US companies who will be guiding and directing that summer's crop of interns. Listening is a big focus of what we work on.

The morning of the training Sara stood out in her enthusiasm. She seemed to be soaking it all in and anticipating the joys of changing a young person's life. We started the session with a basic "getting to know you" scenario. Sara was teamed up with D'Andre, a nineteen-year-old DSY alumnus—one of many who graduate from the program and then return as volunteers to assist in whatever way they can. He was looking forward to helping new supervisors learn how to relate to kids like him by putting himself back in the shoes of his first day at his own internship. Sara had worked on a list of questions she was sure would lead to the beginning of a beautiful relationship and open the door to her intern's bright, shining future.

"Welcome, D'Andre," she said in a super-cheerful voice to start the scene. "My name is Sara and I'll be your supervisor. You're going to be working in our marketing department. Let's start by getting to know each other. Where do you live?"

D'Andre looked down and mumbled, barely audible, "South Side."

Sara looked both surprised and disappointed by D'Andre's tepid response. So she tried a little harder. "Great," she said, more loudly. "So what year of school are you in?"

D'Andre, again quietly, said, "I just graduated."

"Cool! You probably partied hard that night!" she exclaimed, shimmying her shoulders as she spoke. D'Andre shrugged and smiled weakly. Then he looked away, tapping his fingers nervously.

"What was your favorite subject?" Sara tried.

D'Andre looked down again. Hesitantly he said, "Uh, English, I guess."

"Awesome!" She powered on. "Mine was math…Now, what are your hobbies?"

"Um. I like to rap."

"Great!" Sara said. "I do yoga. Do you ever do yoga?"

D'Andre shook his head. He sat silently, looking down at the floor. Another awkward moment passed, and finally Sara broke the silence. "Okay!" she said brightly. "Let's get you started!"

"And...cut," I said.

Sara put her head in her hands and started to moan. D'Andre looked up and smiled at her and touched her shoulder. "Don't worry, Sara. You're new at this."

You can probably sense that this conversation didn't go so well. When Sara wasn't firing off prepackaged, bubbly questions from her "Question List," she seemed to be talking *at* D'Andre, and not taking in and noticing what he was doing, saying, or experiencing. She also was performing as if they were buddies, and they were not. Nor should they have been— she was his boss at his first "real" job.

After D'Andre comforted Sara, we asked her if she noticed that he was playing a young person who was very shy and feeling uncomfortable. Sara said, "Oh, yes! He was totally uncomfortable...and so was I!" When I asked her what she did in response to this discomfort, she said, "I had no idea what to do. I just tried to keep plowing ahead."

I asked D'Andre what he thought. He said, "Before DSY, I would've probably thought she was just a crazy white lady, no offense. But because I've been through DSY, I know that she was just trying to help and be nice. But in the scene, she didn't seem to notice that I wasn't saying much, that I felt funny and put on the spot, and I really didn't know what she was talking about." Then he paused and turned to Sara. "Maybe you could've asked me what I was nervous about, since you knew that I was. Maybe that could've made a difference."

So Many Ways to Have a Lousy Conversation

There's a lot to say about all the issues and challenges in this conversation. Sara and D'Andre come from very different places socially, economically, and culturally, which is part and parcel of the All Stars' and DSY's mission. That means getting people from very different walks of life to hear and talk with one another—a tall order. I'm not going to get on a soapbox here, but given the racial and economic divisions that persist in this country, I think it's an order whose time is well overdue.

The fact is, these disconnects and challenges happen all the time in many of our conversations, even when we're from the same or similar backgrounds. For example, we often have an agenda in advance. In Sara's case, it was a well-meaning "Question List." But once she found herself in the conversation with a real person, that list didn't match the scene, the circumstance, or the actual relationship. Even though the cues were perfectly visible and hearable to her (just like they are to all of us so much of the time, like when the other person checks the time, gives us short answers, stifles a yawn, gets irritated, cuts us off, etc.), Sara stuck tenaciously to her (now-irrelevant) script, character, and agenda. It can be frightening to do anything else, to take the risk to break from your script and actually *be* with the person you're with. That requires listening in new and different ways—being open and curious, perhaps vulnerable, and beginning to co-create with the other person.

Here's another common communication mismatch: You say what you have to say, I say what I have to say, and so it goes. Back and forth. It's like dueling monologues in which both parties are breathing the same air but might as well be by themselves. Sometimes the net result is that they don't connect, or understand, or produce much of anything worthwhile even though they're talking together. Sometimes the result is even worse: Tension, animosity, or emotional upset takes center stage.

Then there's the belief that in a conversation our point of view is the most important thing we can express. I'm all for people expressing their views—in this book I'm doing just that—but sometimes (in fact, a lot of the time) making *that* the priority at the expense of the other person and the relationship is not the best thing to do. Insisting on *my* point of view can be unhealthy and destructive (even self-destructive) at times.

And sometimes a conversation is more like a waiting game, as each person formulates whatever they want to say regardless of what was just said. It's transactional, even when the substance of the conversation isn't a transaction.

What do all of these communication dead ends have in common? Nobody's listening. That's why I call listening a "revolutionary" way to have a conversation. I want to overthrow all of these lousy ways and bring listening—as a creative and collaborative activity—to the forefront. *Viva el escuchando!*

"Can you please look at me and not the teleprompter?"

How Do I Listen? Let Me Count the Ways

While we all know it's a good idea to listen—and that most people don't—*knowing* that fact never made anybody a better listener. The sad truth is that most of us just don't know how. As former CEO Lee Iacocca said, "I only wish I could find an institute that teaches people how to listen. Businesspeople need to listen at least as much as they need to talk."

And so what does it mean to really listen? Let me start with what listening *is not*: Listening is not transactional; listening is not passive; listening is not waiting your turn to talk. Listening *is* active. It's curious. It's creative. It's collaborative.

And listening is a performance.

Just as we can perform as a bicycle rider, a friend, a dad, a team player, an adviser, or a leader, we can perform as a listener. And performing as a listener has everything to do with improvisation. Chapter 7 is all about improvisation, the fifth fundamental of the Becoming Principle. But the connection between improv and listening is so important, I want to get a jump on it here.

If you've ever seen improv comedy performed, you've experienced the kind of magic that takes place as talented people perform what looks and sounds like a very funny, well-rehearsed script. But there is no script. No rehearsal. No plan. And, frankly, it's not magic (although it is magical). Improvisers can create theater without a script for one reason: *They are awesome listeners.* And improvisers perform listening in a very particular way. We listen to build with others. We listen to create with others. We listen to collaborate with others. That's the whole kit and caboodle. It's like active listening on steroids. Improvisers are open and willing to say yes to their co-performers, follow them anywhere, and co-create with everything they are given. We call this act of listening *hearing offers.*

Stephen Nachmanovitch, the improvisational violinist and author of *Free Play*, elegantly explains how conversation and improvisation are so intimately related: "The most common form of improvisation is ordinary speech. As we talk and listen, we are drawing on a set of building blocks (vocabulary) and rules of combining them (grammar). These have been given to us by our culture. But the sentences we make with them may never have been said before and may never be said again. Every conversation is a form of jazz. The activity of instantaneous creation is as ordinary to us as breathing."

In jazz improvisation, the ensemble members (i.e., the people in the band) are listening and building with the notes, the rhythm, the volume, the emotion—what I call musical offers. In ordinary speech, the ensemble members (i.e., the people in the conversation) listen and build with offers that are in the forms of words, emotions, body language, nonverbal sounds, and intent. We make offers all the time, and we are given offers all the time. If we don't hear, see, and build with these offers, then there's just no music.

Say you're meeting with a potential client and you've prepared a fifty-page presentation deck with graphs and data and photos and analysis and numbers and branding. You're feeling pretty good. You've worked hard to get your foot in the door and it's showtime. And there you are, ten minutes into your presentation, and your client yawns. He surreptitiously glances at his phone. But you power on because you've got thirty-seven slides to go, and you're getting to the really good ones that you and your team worked on for days. Your client shifts in his seat a few times, looks at his watch.

This is an offer!

It's practically screaming in your face and jumping up and down in front of you. Please, please, hear it, see it, and build with it. Perhaps you say something like, "Mauricio, let me pause here for a minute to see how we're doing. The deck is here and we can review further at any point, but how does this sound so far?" Mauricio will no longer be yawning, I guarantee that. Mauricio feels heard, included, and attended to in that moment. I can't say what will happen next (the music remains to be made), but at least you have a fighting chance. At least you've heard the offer and you and Mauricio are in the same scene.

In every conversation, we're presented with all kinds of offers. Even if the opposite appears to be the case, like Mauricio's yawn. A colleague ignoring your question is an offer. Your team getting the research that you asked for done early is an offer. A client saying she's not interested in whatever you have to sell is an offer. A laugh at your joke is an offer. Your boss not looking up at you when you come into her office is an offer. The barely audible answers D'Andre performed in response to Sara's overwhelming questions in the training were offers. She just didn't recognize them as such, and she's not alone.

What happens to most of us is that, like Sara, we ignore the offers that are right there, smack in front of us. There are many reasons why this is so. Perhaps we're afraid that we don't know what to do with what we're seeing and hearing, and so we just keep doing what we always do, even as we see the conversation crumble before our eyes. Or we disagree with what we hear, and we put all our energy into mounting a convincing argument. Or we get attached to the locomotive of our agenda and can't get off that train. Or we're worried we'll sound stupid, be inappropriate, say the wrong thing, freeze, or be culturally insensitive. Maybe we're confused. Or annoyed. Upset. Maybe we're caught up in the Knowing Paradigm that we discussed earlier: *Unless I know what to do, I can't do it.*

All of the above are probably true for all of us, some of the time. But armed with the improviser's "superpowers" of performing as a listener, hearing offers and building with them (which you'll come to know as "Yes, and" in chapter 7), we can move into the unknown and unknowable and co-create with another person. All kinds of possibilities and opportunities emerge that are simply not there—until you build them.

Being in the Same Scene

Sara made it through the intern supervisor training, and on the first day of the real internship, a sixteen-year-old named Lavon reported to her. Lavon arrived early, and after a quick hello, Sara invited him into her office. She thought about D'Andre and what he had said to her. She thought about hearing and accepting offers. She remembered to breathe, and when she took a close look at Lavon, she could see he was a bit overwhelmed. Sara sat down, invited him to sit, and was warm and professional.

"Welcome, Lavon. It's great to meet you. I'm Sara, and I'm going to be your supervisor for the next six weeks. How was your commute here this morning?"

"Good," Lavon said quietly.

"I noticed you got to the office early. That's probably a good thing to do for a while as you get used to the commute."

"Yes, ma'am."

Sara noticed her own nervousness and took another breath. "I imagine this might be a bit overwhelming for you. Is this your first job in a corporate office building?"

"Yes," Lavon said, looking down.

"Do you feel nervous?" Sara asked.

Lavon looked up with surprise. She'd nailed it on the head. Quietly, he said, "A little."

Lavon's genuine response buoyed Sara, and she felt her body relax. The peppy edge was gone from her voice when she said, "Well, that makes total sense to me. I remember the first job I ever had in a big office building like this. I was pretty scared."

"You were?"

Both Sara and Lavon were more engaged with each exchange. "Terrified. I was afraid I would be late and got there two hours early."

Lavon smiled. "I got here one hour early. I was worried I was going to be late, too. I'm not terrified, though, ma'am. Just a little nervous."

"So," Sara said, "tell me what you're nervous about. And I'll see if I can help. And then we'll take it from there and get you started. Okay? And please call me Sara." She smiled and reached out her hand.

"Thank you, Sara." Lavon smiled back and shook her hand timidly.

Now we're talking. Er, I mean, listening.

The Power of Silence

My colleagues and I led a workshop on the "art of listening" recently that was attended by a mix of senior executives from financial services, fashion, technology, publishing, and consumer products companies. They were all folks at the top of their game, most of whom would be considered gifted conversationalists but not necessarily great listeners. That's what they came to work on.

Our job in this workshop was to help these accomplished people *perform* as listeners. So we led them in an exercise we created called "Amazing Silence." Here's what happens: Two people sit in chairs facing each other. They begin by taking a few seconds to silently look at each other directly in the eyes. Then one person begins by sharing something that's important to him, perhaps that he wouldn't normally share in a work context, in no more than one or two sentences, while maintaining direct eye contact. Before the other person responds, they are both instructed to sit for ten to fifteen seconds in total silence while continuing to hold that eye contact. Then the other person responds with a statement or a question, in one or two sentences. And again, before the other person responds, they both sit facing each other for another ten to fifteen seconds of eye contact in total silence. Back and forth they go like this for about three to four minutes.

As my fellow POAL trainers and I walked around the room during these conversations, we found that many people were looking at the ground, or the space right next to their partners' heads—anywhere but right in the eyes. We coached them to keep looking at each other, despite its difficulty. Once they got through the initial embarrassment, they settled into a slow, intense, and immediately intimate conversation together. After the first four minutes we switched roles: The original speaker became the listener and vice versa.

We discussed with the participants what they had just experienced. With their partners, they had talked about everything from worry about parents or children, to sadness about illness or loss and workplace stress, to excitement about new opportunities or falling in love.

We also heard strong responses to the exercise, including:

"Wow. I had no idea I was going to go there."

"This was hard."

"Oh my God! This was the most intimate conversation I've had in years!"

"This was wonderful."

"Ugh. This was really weird."

"I learned so much about what my partner is going through. I feel so much empathy."

"Are you telling us to do this at work?"

As for the last comment: No, I'm not telling you to do this at work! (Although you certainly could if you want to.) This is an exercise that awakens and stretches your capacity to slow down, listen, make a connection with another human being, and talk sparingly in an intimate, direct, and empathetic way. In this particular workshop, where almost nobody knew anybody else, people were shocked by how quickly they came to know the person they sat across from. "We never allow this to happen," our fashion executive said, "to be that trusting and vulnerable at work." Others described it as creating a space for connecting with another human being, and some talked about how being listened to and looked at in this way made them more thoughtful and open in what they shared. The publishing exec said it was "hard to be looked at so intently. I felt like I was being seen…I realize that's hard for me. To be seen by others."

To see, and to be seen by others. To hear, and to be heard by others. In this exercise, people's silence, eye contact, and sharing of something important was a way to perform, and thereby create, intimacy. And through this activity, we were implicitly asking participants not to listen *for* anything. Listening *for* something can limit what we hear, leading us to assume we know what's to come, what's important or unimportant, and that we understand. And these assumptions cause us to miss the range of offers that are before and around us. On a personal level, listening *for* can cause us to block out, distort, or dismiss another human being. On a business level, it's a barrier to relationship building, opportunity, innovation, and potential success.

Nix the Script

Kerri, an SVP at an insurance company, contacted us in the hope that the company, already an industry leader, could continue to break through the sad reputation so eloquently articulated by director Woody Allen: "There are worse things in life than death. Have you ever spent an evening with an insurance salesman?"

Kerri was looking to raise her salespeople's game by growing them as listeners, communicators, and collaborators with their clients. Sevanne Kassarjian, a most insightful and talented POAL coach/director (and salesperson), led our work with this team.

"What do you need help with?" she asked them. "What are some client relationships or conversations that you find challenging?"

Tom, a senior sales manager for their southern region, shot his arm up. "I got a call a few days ago that I need help with. Pick me!" he pleaded. After good-natured laughing and clapping from his colleagues, he explained his challenge. A potential client wanted a free trial of one of their risk-insurance products. But even though the company doesn't give free trials, he was concerned that he might not have clearly conveyed that. Not knowing how to handle the situation, Tom hadn't called the client back. When he got an e-mail from the client (the evening before this session) saying she had hired an analyst to start using the product and was calling him to get her free trial, he panicked. He knew he needed to talk to the client...but how?

Sevanne brought Tom onstage to improvise the conversation, with her playing "Ella," the client. In the first run-through, Ella talked fast and forcefully, expressing that she needed to get started with the free trial of the product—now.

Tom responded, "Ella, let me first say that you are an important customer to us and we really value your business. And so I'll get back to you on that."

The scene was over in seconds.

Sevanne turned to the group and asked them what they heard. People were practically jumping up and down to respond. Roscoe, a fellow salesperson, said, "Yuck. That's what I sound like, too. Tom's using our script about how much he values the client but he just wants to get out of this conversation, fast. I feel for you, man."

Kerri said, "You were placating her and probably pissing her off."

Sevanne pointed out one of the offers that the client made to Tom: It was the offer of urgency—she really needed this free trial to happen *ASAP*. She asked the group, "What would it look like to let the offer really land?"

Andy, a soft-spoken, more junior person, said, "We need to find out more. Why is it so urgent?"

Tom was hesitant. "If I go down that path, she's going to think that I can give her the free trial!"

Sevanne added, "Do both. Find out about the urgency *and* tell her that the free trial is a no-go. But most important, perform as someone who really wants to help your client."

In the next scene, Tom was visibly more relaxed. He opened with, "Look, Ella, first I want to apologize for the time it's taken for me to get back to you. I heard in your last message how important this was. What's happening on your side?"

"My CEO wasn't sold on the product. But this free trial is the way to sell him."

"Oh, I see. What do *you* think about the product?"

"I love it. I think this is the way to go."

Tom looked shocked. He broke character, paused, turned to Sevanne for help.

Syreeta, the customer relationship data manager, called out from the audience, "Keep going! Find out more! And tell her we don't do free trials!"

Tom swallowed hard and then turned back to "Ella." "Well, that's great to hear. So, a few things: I want to hear more about what you're seeing from your vantage point. That could help us to figure out together what to do next, because, well, a free trial of this product is not something I can offer to you, although I wish I could. Can we figure this out together?"

"Oh! I didn't realize that. Would you be willing to do a quick call with my CEO then? I think I can convince him to sit down with you briefly, but I need some talking points to make my case."

"Okay, let me pull some together for you. I can do that by end of day today—I know this is urgent. How's that sound?"

The room was abuzz with chatter and applause when Sevanne ended the scene. "This became a partnering conversation!" Roscoe exclaimed. "Listening and collaborating with the client is a hell of a lot better than reciting the line, 'You are a valued partner.'"

Having dumped his script and the catchphrases, Tom was able to make an actual connection with Ella. It became obvious to him—and everybody in the room—that these phrases were doing the exact opposite of their intent: They were actually *devaluing* the customer. I'm not against scripts, especially if you regularly work to write new ones that are helpful and specific to the situation you're in. But being scripted by default, instead of listening and building with offers from real people in the moment, can take you nowhere fast.

Curiosity Doesn't Kill

Toward the end of the discussion following the scene, Andy raised his hand shyly and asked if Sevanne had a list of questions he could use in situations like this. Other people's faces lit up expectantly, so Sevanne was gentle with her answer. "Here's the thing, Andy," she said. "I'll give you some examples of questions that could help—but I don't want to just give you another script. Tom's questions to Ella came from a very specific kind of improvisational response to the client's offer—he responded with a performance of *curiosity*."

Of course, the first time through his scene, Tom wasn't curious at all—he felt backed into a corner. And that's where the *performance* of curiosity comes in. Many of the offers that come our way—especially when we're trying to influence someone, or make a sale, or when we disagree—are not what we were hoping to hear. So while your "natural" response might be any number of things—arguing, convincing, disappearing, saying it again but louder—how do you accept an offer and build with it? Be curious. And it's not just salespeople who benefit from curiosity. When author Daniel Pink says (via the title of his excellent book), "To sell is human," what he means is that we're *all* in sales. If you can engage your curiosity about these offers, you can turn even the most awkward, uncomfortable, or unpleasant conversations into productive ones.

Our go-to exercise for overcoming the curiosity-deadening impact of "unwelcome offers" is called "Performing Curiosity." We give pairs of people a topic on which they disagree. Person B starts by making a statement about the topic, and Person A must respond to this (and to anything that follows) with a "curious" question, meaning the question must:

1. Be open (not multiple choice or answerable by yes or no).
2. Be connected to whatever was just said (i.e., it picks up on an "offer").
3. Not be a statement of opinion disguised as a question.

Sound easy? It's not. Here's an example of a health-conscious A who's definitely struggling:

B: I think soda manufacturers have every right to sell their sugary drinks in schools.
A: Do you think cigarette companies should sell theirs, too?

Uh-oh. Three strikes: (1) It's a closed question; (2) it moves away from the offer of sugary drinks; and (3) it wears its point of view like a banner being carried into battle.

Here's how I direct the A's: Listen carefully, and when your partner finishes, take a breath and avoid starting with the words *Do* or *Don't*. Instead, start with *Why, How, Who, Where,* or *What.* Those are the words curious people use! And even if you *hate* what they are saying and don't feel curious about it, if you do what curious people do—if you *perform* curiosity—you might still hate (or a slightly modified version of hate) what they're saying, but you won't hate them. Big difference.

And that's what happens. Here's our pair again, with A performing curiosity:

B: I think soda manufacturers have every right to sell their sugary drinks in schools.

A: Why?

B: A number of reasons, but primarily because in my experience, prohibiting things that kids enjoy just makes them "forbidden fruit"—actually that much more appealing.

A: How have you experienced that?

B: When I was growing up, my mom never let a drop of soda pop into the house. When we asked about it, she'd go off on a rant about how unhealthy it was. So my brother and I became obsessed. We'd buy bottles of Coke and bury them in the backyard. I'd spend every cent of my allowance on soda—and candy, which was also forbidden. Once I left home, sugar became my number one food group, and I became diabetic at nineteen.

A: Oh. Wow. I'm sorry to hear that. Why was your mom so vehement about it?

So in response to curious questions, B says some things that A wasn't expecting. The A's find themselves actually getting to know the B's. The conversation moves away from argument or convincing and toward understanding and relationship building, and an array of possibilities becomes available.

Sevanne spoke with Tom the week after the workshop. He had finally gotten back to Ella, and it had gone better than he expected. By dumping his confining script, he partnered with his client and came up with a solution that went beyond simply closing the sale. They really did meet together with her boss, who was impressed with her forward thinking. Tom's value to Ella grew—not just as a vendor, but as a consultant. Or to use more artistic language, they co-created, improvised, and made some music together.

Playing with Disagreements

Vera is a successful senior director at a midsized software development company. Theo is an ambitious developer turned client project manager. Together, they had secured a big new job with a communications giant they had been working with for some time. Vera was responsible for the overall relationship with the client across all of the various projects that the company did for them. Theo ran this particular project and managed their team. The time had come to prepare for the launch of this new phase of work.

Vera and Theo had rubbed each other the wrong way for a long time. They had frequent miscommunication and conflicts between their respective styles. Vera called me after a particularly bad week for their relationship. They had gotten into a fight over an impromptu meeting that Theo had held with the client team. It was, in effect, a project launch meeting that was premature (in Vera's opinion) and didn't include her. Vera was "fit to be tied" (as my mother used to say, which I never understood, but now I say it all the time). She was furious.

In the months that I had worked with her, I learned that Vera tended to have a short fuse and seemed irritated at people a lot. Theo, on the other hand, was cool and blasé, a laid-back sort of dude. He had a habit of laughing when people got angry at him, which of course infuriated Vera even more. But despite all this, they were one of the company's most successful business cultivation teams. Clients loved them, and they often ended up working together on engagements.

I suggested to Vera that she and Theo do a performance coaching session together with me, which she agreed to. As soon as we got into the conference room, I asked each of them to state their point of view in this disagreement.

Vera began. She was pretty wound up. "Theo, once again, usurped my authority by holding a meeting with the client—didn't invite me to it, didn't tell me about it, and is acting like this isn't a big freaking deal, which it is. *I'm* the relationship manager. I sent the client, Bernard, an e-mail to schedule the project launch meeting, and he wrote back saying that it happened already. I was totally caught off guard and humiliated. Theo does this kind of shit all the time."

Then Theo: "Vera, Vera, relax. We're already under way with the next phase. I'm on the ground with our team and the client. The meeting happened sort of organically. Bernie and I were talking about next steps and before I knew it he called in some of his folks and so I called in the team and we took it from there. It's all good, man. I wish people would just chill a bit around here. Everything is fine. In fact, everything is great."

"Thank you for these performances," I said, giving them both a round of applause. They both turned and glared at me. *Now we're getting somewhere*, I thought. *They agree with each other about being mad at me.*

"For our next performance," I began, "I want to help you to play with this disagreement. I'd like you to perform as the other person. So, Vera, you're going to play Theo; and, Theo, you're going to play Vera. And you're going to take on the point of view that the other person has. I want you to perform this passionately, with conviction, and do your best to really convince me and each other that this is the way you feel. Okay?"

Silence.

Irritable Vera said, "This is ridiculous, Cathy. You are not treating this situation seriously, and I really don't appreciate it."

Laid-back Theo chimed in, "I don't have time to play games. You're wasting our time, dude."

One of the things that makes it hard to listen to people with whom we disagree is that we often take ourselves (me, me, and more me) very, very seriously. I certainly do. *I have been wronged! I am misunderstood! I'm being dissed!* Look, I get it. And I mean no disrespect. You may be "right." I just believe that, sometimes, the way we relate to ourselves and these situations is as if no one else on the planet experiences the same kinds of things a million times a minute. And being right about them doesn't change the situation, apparently. Maybe you (we) *are* right. But so what? And now what?

So anyway, here we were, having a disagreement about how to work on having a disagreement. "Actually, I'm taking you very seriously," I said, acknowledging their offers. "You guys are already playing a game, doing a performance. Is it working for you?"

They both shook their heads no.

"Are you open to what the other one is saying?"

More head shaking, maybe a little chagrin.

"Okay. That's what I want to help you with, so I'm giving you another performance to try. You're in a bad play. It's the *I'm Right and You're Wrong* play. You're both taking yourselves and your positions too seriously, and you're not taking your relationship and the project seriously enough. And that's a performance choice. So let's make another one. Let's play with this disagreement. You with me?"

They looked at each other, turned back to me, and nodded tentatively.

"Great. Now, places, please." I pointed my fingers to show them where to stand (where the other was standing), so as to assume their new characters.

The new performance began. And an interesting thing happened. They each were able to express very convincingly what the other person had been saying. In their new performances of each other they said all the things that the other had said—and added some new ones. They were passionate, articulate, and clearly capable of hearing and listening very well to each other, now that they were performing as each other.

This time when they finished and I started applauding, they clapped along as well. And we all laughed. Tired, they both sat down. "Well, what do we do now?" Theo asked.

Vera turned to him. "I get what you were saying, Theo. I understand how the impromptu meeting happened. You were there in the middle of it all. It makes sense."

Theo nodded and said, "Yeah. I guess I also can see how you felt set up. I probably should've told you that we ended up sitting down with Bernard and the team so you would've known to not send that e-mail."

How'd they get to this place where they could possibly listen to each other? As I said earlier, Vera and Theo had been performing in a lousy play. They were initially, and understandably, reluctant to see it that way. Calling it a performance and a play *immediately* shone a light on the fact that they had choices. And if they had choices—as opposed to *the only possible way that anybody in my situation could conceivably feel*—that meant they could make a different choice from the one they had made.

Vera and Theo, after some serious prodding, chose a playful performance that would help them listen to and hear each other. In order to take on each other's points of view, they had to simultaneously hear and give voice to what the other person was saying, feeling, and experiencing. They didn't have to agree with it. They just needed to perform it. In a way, they were retroactively accepting each other's offers by now being creative with what they had heard. They were playing games (as Theo pointed out) with their disagreements. And it was a game being played on behalf of the relationship and of the project. To play it successfully, they had to momentarily abandon their strongly held positions, and that helped them see and hear a bunch of stuff they couldn't see and hear before.

Be Brave. Be Curious. Be Playful. Be Quiet.

So, to summarize, here are my four favorite ways to listen:

Be brave. As we saw with Sara, the intern supervisor, it takes bravery to wade into waters you might not feel comfortable in. Really hearing and taking in another's point of view shakes up your own status quo.

Be curious. There is almost always more to what you're hearing than meets the ear, as Tom, the insurance man, found out. Performing curiosity in a conversation gives you the chance to be a learner and a grower, rather than a transactional communicator; to hear things you wouldn't normally hear, and to see things—and the person you're talking with— in new ways.

Be playful. Once upon a time, we made up games constantly. The instinct to play runs deep—it's an important part of how we learn—and finding ways to "play with" challenging conversations or disagreements (like Vera and Theo did) can get us unstuck fast.

Be quiet. Resist the urge to talk all the time. Resist the concern that being quiet means you don't have something to say. Take in what your fellow conversationalist is saying. The Amazing Silence exercise gave people a structure for being quiet. Being in the moment with another person. Letting them know you're listening with your roaring silence.

When you listen to all the offers coming your way, you can build and create something new *with* the other person. If you're steadfastly committed to performing in a way that enables the other to be heard, you will help that person to hear *you*. Together you're creating a shared point of view, a shared understanding. Ours, not yours or mine.

But before you start singing "Kumbaya," consider this: Much of what you hear—the offers you now perceive at every turn and work to accept and build with—will not necessarily be what you want. Some of it won't be what anybody wants. Some of it will simply be (excuse my use of the technical term here) crap. What now? Read on to our next fundamental.

Listen!: The Revolutionary Way to Have a Conversation Exercises

1. Pick two meetings and a one-on-one conversation that are upcoming and choose to make listening your priority performance. Try not to listen *for* anything. Pause longer than you normally would before you respond. Make more eye contact than you usually do. Let people see that you are listening.

2. Take special notice of body language offers. How someone sits, her facial expressions, her walk, what she's looking at, and more. Listen, see, and respond to those offers.

3. Take someone else's point of view that you really disagree with. Spend some time—from fifteen minutes to a whole day—in his shoes, holding his opinions. How does he see the world? What do you see differently as a result?

4. Perform curiosity: Do you have a friend or colleague you disagree with about something? Have a conversation in which (for once!) you don't try to convince her she's wrong, but instead find out everything you can about how she sees the topic or issue. Don't assume you know anything.

5. Ask a colleague or friend to tell you a story about himself that you've never heard. Sit back and listen.

Performance Fundamental Four:
Create with Crap

Option A is not available. So let's just kick the shit out
of Option B.

—*Sheryl Sandberg*

A design and innovation consulting firm asked us for some help with an issue that was causing them a lot of grief and consternation. Marcus, one of their principals, was becoming increasingly difficult to work with. He had been there from the start and was considered the consummate artist—an amazing designer, a technical wizard, wildly creative, and all that. But he wasn't much of a team player, and the growth of the company seemed to be both exacerbating his idiosyncrasies and making them harder for the whole team to deal with.

Marcus was also a bit of a snob, had a quick temper, and was prone to negativity. He was cavalier about deadlines, often missed meetings, and blithely made up excuses to cover his ass. He was involved to some degree in a third of the projects under way at any given time, and while the team depended on his work, he couldn't be relied on. As their business expanded, the office environment was becoming increasingly toxic.

The CEO, Colin, was beyond frustrated, and the fact that Marcus was his longtime friend didn't make things any easier. Colin had held many meetings, had countless conversations, had counseled others on how to better handle Marcus. But nothing seemed to be helping. As the year wrapped up, Colin decided to take a more formal approach to Marcus's year-end review. They typically just caught up and reviewed the year over a few beers. This time, he wanted to send a clear message that things must change. He asked Marcus to take a few weeks to write a thorough and as-honest-as-possible self-review. And he set up a review process where they would meet not just once, but a number of times. He gave

Marcus three weeks to submit the review, and he confirmed the deadline to make sure Marcus was cool with it.

The deadline, a Friday, passed with no sign of the review. By Monday it still hadn't hit Colin's in-box, and he was so infuriated he could barely contain himself. What kind of friend would so blatantly disregard what had so obviously been a serious and thoughtful olive branch? Colin wanted to barge in and tell Marcus what a f$#&-up he was, how much chaos he'd created, and how he was no longer welcome in the office.

After several sleepless nights, Colin finally calmed down enough to realize that he owed not Marcus, but himself and the firm, the chance to make one last-ditch effort to try to save their working relationship, or at least to end things well. That's when he brought in POAL to coach him on how to handle the situation.

I felt for both Colin and Marcus (whom, by the way, I really like). While this was a difficult and awkward situation, it was also quite common. More often than not, we have people of mixed talents on our teams. (Just ask *my* team about my long list of "mixed" talents, and you'll get an earful.) We all do some things well and other things not so well. In this case, the not-so-well was kicking the crap out of the well.

"Do you want to keep working with him?" I asked Colin.

He thought about it for a few minutes. "Yes. But I'm worried that might not be possible. Maybe the party is finally over. Maybe Marcus can't do anything other than this." Then he added, "Maybe *I* can't do anything other than this. And it's just not good for the firm, for our clients, or for our friendship. It basically sucks."

I agreed. "It's a really bad situation, no doubt. But how about you take this on as a gift? As a creative challenge?"

Colin looked at me as if I had just grown a second head. "What are you talking about?" he asked. "This situation is a steaming pile of crap! How is that a creative challenge?" It was a very good question.

Lookin' for Creativity in All the Wrong Places

The science-fiction writer Theodore Sturgeon famously said, "Ninety percent of everything is crap." I'm not sure about the actual percentage, but let's agree that a good deal of what we face every day in our work and lives obeys Sturgeon's Law. And if, as the saying goes, what we need to do

"I stopped complaining about people invading my personal space and started renting it out."

in response to being handed all those lemons is to make lemonade, I'm all for it. But in real life, where it's a bit more complex than a bunch of squeezing and a cup of sugar, we all could use a recipe. Calling it a creative challenge sounds great, but *how*?

There are lots of great books and articles on creativity. I've read a lot of them (and listed a few of my favorites in the recommended reading section at the end of this book), and I'm fascinated with their insights into the nature and location of creativity, which resonate with what I've seen vividly through our work at POAL. This includes insights such as:

We're all creative. Not just painters, choreographers, musicians, actors, and designers. Every single human being has the capacity to be creative in a multitude of ways.

Creativity is social. The myth of the lone genius is losing currency as we understand that all creativity builds on what and who came before us, and is further developed by the input of others.

I'd like to add one more: *Creativity applies everywhere.* If we're a creative species, that means we can apply creativity to a wide variety of circumstances. We can be creative in how we live our lives and carry out our work. I'm talking about everything, from how we conduct a meeting to how we raise a family to how we craft a memo to how we walk the dog. This also includes all the crap that surrounds us and that we deal with all the time.

Creating with the "crap" is what I want to focus on in this chapter. Can we take our collective creativity and bring it more consciously and more productively into everyday life and work? Can we create something out of the nasty arguments between colleagues, the disrespectful attitude of a boss or peers, the e-mail system that insists on going over quota with no warning, our impatience with the mistakes of a subordinate, our own belief that everyone else is the problem?

The answer is yes (and yes and yes and yes . . .). Through performance, we can create new ways of thinking, new emotions, new language, new characters, and new ideas via new scenes and new plays.

Creating the New Play

When I explained all this to Colin, he was skeptical but open. Certainly, *fixing* the problem hadn't worked, so he'd be willing to give *creating with it* a shot. So we got started, looking at what it would take to "remount" his company's play; looking at the characters and the roles they play, reworking or cutting the scenes that don't work, and maybe adding some new ones. I brought in my close colleague and POAL co-founder, David Nackman, to help me. He's a first-class director, and I knew he could be helpful in our mix.

The first character to reshape was not Marcus's but Colin's. He had to play the part of Marcus's boss, not his friend. And as Marcus's boss, Colin had to do some uncomfortable directing that included narrowing the scope of Marcus's responsibilities and putting him on probation for two months.

Colin then had to look at his current cast to see what they had all been doing to enable Marcus's crappy performance. "All of you have participated in creating this situation," we told Colin. "That doesn't mean Marcus is off the hook—not at all—but you need to own some of this because you and the company have played a part in producing this failure. And when you meet with Marcus to read him the riot act and put him on probation, you need to let him know that you know that, and you're not going to participate in it anymore."

David came up with an idea for creatively impacting on a common—and problematic—scene. Remember the series *The Office*, the original British version from 2001? They were the first TV show to use the (now somewhat overused) "mockumentary" device of having characters talk about their thoughts and feelings to an unseen and unheard interviewer after a scene. David thought they could add the same device to their drama—literally adding short "interview" scenes to the work process in which they could turn to each other and, in front of an imaginary close-up camera, reflect on what had just happened, how they felt about it, and what they thought should or could happen next. We talked with Colin, Marcus, and some of the key players about the idea. And a couple of days later, this happened:

> **Siddhartha** (*wrapping up a call with Marcus*): Okay, man. Can we review these design changes tomorrow morning? I figure we need about thirty minutes. Say, nine forty-five? Ten?
>
> **Marcus** (*typing intently into his online calendar*): I don't know…Lemme look at my morning…I have an eleven o'clock, and I figure the changes will take a couple of hours, but I'll move it as fast as I can and shoot for a quarter of.
>
> **Siddhartha** (*typing intently into his own calendar*): Cool.
> **Marcus:** Got it.

The next morning at ten, Siddhartha had not heard from Marcus. He texted him: "Wuz up? R u calling me?"

"Yup…10:45."

Siddhartha texted back: "WHAT??? WE SAID 9:45…we need at least 30 mins…10:45 too tight." When Marcus called Siddhartha five minutes later, Siddhartha was so annoyed he could barely pay attention, Marcus was highly defensive (and the design changes were only half done), and they were both dumbfounded.

I'd call this a crappy conversation, no?

Three hours later, Marcus was sitting in the office of a colleague, Jessica, who was in on the *Office* device. He was in the middle of an

Office-style monologue. "It's like being in a bad dream that happens over and over," he said. Like a good interviewer, Jessica focused on him attentively, nodding appreciatively as he spoke.

"And it's always the same: At the end of the conversation, we both think we know what we agreed to do, but when the time comes to do whatever it was, it's like we were in two different conversations. And these days, I'm really trying! I write everything down! By the time we get off the phone, I've written a blow-by-blow description of what needs to be done and when..." Marcus trailed off, a look of enlightenment suddenly appearing on his face. "Which I should probably share with Siddhartha, to make sure he agrees that it's what we said."

"And, cut," Jessica said.

And starting with his next meeting, that's what Marcus did. It wasn't the most novel idea. But you have to understand something. Marcus *never* did anything like any of this. One, he actually reflected on what transpired. Two, he went to a colleague to get some help. Three, he came up with a new work process. Four, it's working—for now. Siddhartha and Marcus have been staying in sync and not at each other's throats. And what made it possible was the small but powerful creative leap of turning the crap that was driving everybody crazy into a sitcom monologue.

Working on the How

Einstein said, "Play is the highest form of research." I couldn't agree more. That's why we had Colin, Marcus, and the rest of the team embark on a playful, creative experiment in which they began to look beyond the *results* (aka the problems, the situation, the "crap") and shifted their focus to the *how*—how they were producing the dysfunction together. And then, *how* might their workflow, priorities, and division of labor be reorganized? *How* might their conversations, emotional responses, and questions change?

This work was an unfamiliar mix of play and performance *and* hard, thoughtful, and tedious work. For example, to mitigate the hyper-speedy environment of their overcapacity business, they instituted what they called "slow-motion replay" mode in meetings—at any point, anybody could ring a chime on their phone, after which everyone would take a deep breath, together. They'd then slowly begin to review the past few minutes of the meeting, working to carefully figure out what was on the critical path and make very clear how pieces of the work were to be executed. Colin worked with the managers to implement a new job-tracking system. When the "mockumentary" device got tiresome, Alicia, a senior designer, suggested a weekly contest for who most frequently asked and then facilitated the process question ("How is this going?") every week. To everyone's surprise, Marcus won once.

Together with the POAL team, they were carefully and playfully deconstructing and reconstructing their process of work, conversations, relationships, and values. Marcus, who forced all of this in the first place, had become quite philosophical about it. "When Colin called me into his office after I didn't make my performance review deadline, I felt like it was the worst day of my life," Marcus confessed to me. "I was so freakin' humiliated and angry. I honestly had never given any attention to the team—I was pretty much only into and looking at what *I* was doing. *My* deliverable. But one thing that became clear since then is that there's a lot that goes into working effectively as a team that is actually part of a creative process."

Process over Product

As someone who has spent a lot of my life in the theater, I can tell you that the heart and soul of any production is not the final show the audience sees. It's the hundreds of hours of creativity that go into producing it. When you go to see *The Lion King*, you marvel at how effortlessly beautiful everything appears. But that's only because the cast, crew, and creative team spent months engaged in what might be considered extremely mundane and boring work. Weeks of focusing solely on how to move around the stage. Weeks on entrances and exits. More weeks practicing the same scene, over and over again. Days of fittings, standing stock-still for measurements, plaster casts, tucks, and pins. The actors rehearse and rehearse and rehearse, discovering new ways of presenting their theatrical product in collaboration with a huge team. It's a given in the theater that the process leading up to the big performance is not just necessary but is where the creative action is. The show literally won't and can't go on without it.

Understandably, in business we're all very focused on the results, and I love results as much as the next person. Who doesn't want to find a cure for cancer, get a return on an investment, or fix our educational system? But if we get seduced by a results-only point of view, we lose sight of the social and creative process that actually gets us to the desired results. A fabulous meal at the dinner table doesn't just appear. It's not just the chef concocting an amazing array of tastes, smells, textures, and visual presentation that makes us ooh, ahh, and say, "Yummy!" People planted the seeds, milked the cows, picked the vegetables, drove the trucks, flew the planes, packed up the produce, designed the supermarket stands, analyzed the pricing, experimented with previous recipes, produced the cookware, and felled the trees. You're probably getting my point by now. The mundane, human *process of creating*—whatever the results—needs to come out of the closet, see the light of day, be celebrated, studied, developed, highlighted, and explored.

Indeed, process and result can't be separated, even though the latter is emphasized in our culture. When we emphasize product, it gets in the way of our collective ability to see how things are made and that, again, *we* are the makers. We are not only consumers of products and of our culture, we are the *creators* of products and culture. And that includes crap! Rather than act like crap must be avoided, ignored, and reviled, let's recognize that we created the crap, and that we can therefore create *with* the crap.

Colin and Marcus were both only results-oriented, to the detriment of the process. Colin could see only "problem child" Marcus. Marcus could see only his "stellar" creative results, unaware of and uninterested in the path of wreckage he was producing along the way. Once they both (along with the rest of the team) took this all on as a creative challenge, the results naturally came into line in a way that they hadn't even approached when they were looking at the results only. The quality of their work product for clients improved. Significantly. Projects were delivered on time, with room to spare. People weren't walking around furious or demoralized. They felt energized. Marcus began to support and mentor younger designers. Colin began sleeping again.

Back to the Ensemble

Remember the insight *Creativity is social* that I mentioned earlier in this chapter? As you probably already know if you're reading a book like this, there is plenty of research that now supports this idea, and it's addressed in numerous TED talks, academic and popular books, and classrooms the world over. And yet we still cling to the myth of the lone genius, personified by people like Marcus. In the businesses I visit every day, most people still believe that creativity happens only when gifted and talented individuals are off in a cabin somewhere far, far away from the rest of humanity.

When we hear the phrase "creative impulse," we just don't tend to think of a team or a group. There must be some kind of a muse sprinkling fairy dust on these brilliant individuals as creativity springs out of them. But particularly when it comes to business (though honestly I think this is true across the board), the creative impulse almost always happens collectively, even when it appears to spring from one individual. Just as the theater sheds light on process over product, it also sheds light on ensemble over individual creativity. When creativity becomes an improvisational performance, it is de facto social. There's a whole cast, crew, and audience who make the performance possible. Stars are born not by solo performances with no one there to see them but through a combination of players on and off the set. The greatest performances are never singular acts. When we make the conscious choice to perform creativity, together we make the messes and together we make the solutions.

Do Try This at Home

After my final session with Colin and his team, Alicia (the designer who created the "how" contest) approached me and somewhat shyly asked if any of this "creating with crap" could be used at home. "Please do!" I said.

A few weeks later I got the following e-mail:

To: Cathy Salit
Fr: Alicia Brownell
Re: Oh, Crap

My husband is very punctual when it comes to getting to work, but when it comes to meeting up at a movie or getting somewhere for the kids, he's habitually late. This really annoys me, and he just stares into space when I call him on it. It's been going on for years. I decided to try to be creative for a change after our POAL session a few weeks ago. I told him that I wanted to try a new performance about his lateness because I was frustrated and bored with the one

I was doing. I asked him if we could make a rule where any time that he was late, he had to pay me back by dancing with me for 5 minutes that evening (I love to dance, he likes to sometimes). He thought I had lost my mind. I frankly thought I had, too. Why should I reward him for being late? But I knew I had to at least try something new.

Anyway, last Saturday he was late three times, and so we danced that evening for 15 minutes after dinner. It felt weird and awkward and then we just started laughing and dancing and laughing some more. We had the best time! And I wasn't annoyed with him afterward. It's the strangest thing I've ever done. I hope I can keep it up, or if not, keep coming up with new creative ideas. Thanks! ☺

Alicia figured out a way to take an upsetting, dull, crappy problem and pair it with an inspired, beautiful, humorous act of creativity. Imagine if we could all dance more and be annoyed less.

What I love about Alicia's story is that it shows just how amazingly transformative creativity can be. And the more we create, the more practiced at creativity we become. So whether it's how we respond to a colleague's inability to deliver on time or a spouse's inability to show up to a date on time—we can make the problem go away. Vanish. Change the entirety of what is happening. Build with our individual and collective crap... to grow and create change.

Okay. You've chosen to grow, you're building ensembles, hearing and building with offers, and creating with crap. So far so good. To do all that, you've been performing your heart out—you've been improvising. Improvisation (*improv* in the United States and *impro* everywhere else) is itself a fundamental of performance so important it could have its own book. (In fact, it has many, and I suggest you read some of the ones I've listed in the recommended reading section.) As a crucial part of the Becoming Principle, I'm going to urge you to improvise your life, and to find out how, just keep reading.

Create with Crap Exercises

1. The next time somebody says or does something that you think is stupid, irrelevant, or problematic, write a poem, draw a cartoon, or make up a song about it.

2. Following Professor Einstein's advice, bring a group of people together (your team, a few colleagues—or this could be a job for your personal board of performance directors) to "research" a toxic environment or situation at work—by playing with it. Create a short melodramatic play about it. Include scenes where you explore the mundane process—conversations, attitudes, decisions—that produced the crappy situation.

3. The next time you're having an argument with your significant other or a friend, ask him to dance instead.

4. Be on the lookout for the crap you're giving to others. Since we mostly think we're right, or that less-than-optimal things we do are justifiably in response to something else (which could very well be), it can be hard to see. But at least on a few occasions, notice your crap and then tell people, "I really did a bunch of crap today. Got any ideas about how to be creative with it?"

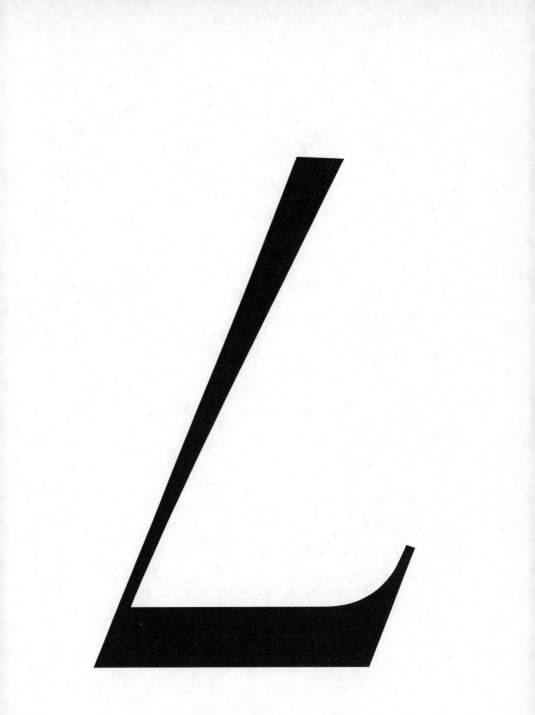

Performance Fundamental Five:
Improvise Your Life

Life is a lot like jazz. It's best when you improvise.
                                        —*George Gershwin*

I've been performing improv comedy for almost twenty-five years. But I'm a high-strung gal, so even with all this experience, every time I'm about to go onstage with my ensemble, the Proverbial Loons, I become a runaway train of neuroses. My brain runs through the same tired, old script: *I can't improvise...I haven't practiced enough...I can't improvise...I won't remember anything from scene to scene because tonight's the night that early-onset dementia will finally kick in...I can't improvise...*

In an attempt to stop this loop of insanity, I have developed a "performance before the performance" that does the trick. Minutes before the show, I grab my dear friend and fellow Loon Marian Rich and pull her into the nearby 7-Eleven. Marian and I have performed together for three decades. She is a consummate improviser, a delight to perform with, and very patient with me. I grab her arm. "Can I talk to you for a minute?"

She rolls her eyes. "Can't improvise?"

"Yes," I say, trying hard not to totally lose my shit. "Marian, I think I don't have it anymore."

She looks at me with love...and irritation. "Cathy," she says firmly, "we've done this little performance of yours so many times before. You always do fine!"

"Yes, but..."

"*Yes, and,* Cathy. May I remind you that the golden rule of improv is to say yes to everything?"

"I know. I know," I say. "I'm just worried I'll be terrible."

"It's not about you. It's about us, the ensemble. Your job is to make *the rest of us* look good, remember?"

"Yes," I admit. "*And* I'm still probably going to mess up the show structure..."

"*Fantastic*," she roars, and the cashier looks up with concern. "Can't wait to see and *celebrate* your mistakes. Nothing like a curveball to inspire us to become more creative."

This is all starting to sound familiar, but my heart is still pounding. "But," I say, and she raises a meaningful eyebrow. I correct myself. "*And*...I'm scared. What if I wind up in a scene and don't know what I'm doing?"

She points a banana at me and I flash on a hundred years of comedy. "Best thing that could happen," she says. "Follow your fear. *Go into the cave.* That's where you grow as an artist and as a person."

I'm feeling calmer. Everything Marian has told me makes sense, and I'm beginning to look forward to the show. I thank her profusely. She smiles. "I'm just following your lead. Doing my bit with your bit." She pauses. "You know where I learned all this, right?" she asks.

I know what she's going to say.

"From you, you dope! These are the tenets of improv *you* teach!"

Some of this scene may be a little exaggerated, but not much. (There was no banana.) Marian has led me through the tenets of improv, one by one, that are the backbone of "professional" improvisation wherever it's done. I want to delve into them with you now, not because I want or expect you to become an improv comedian but because *everything* about the Becoming Principle in this book—when you're being who you are and who you're becoming, when you're performing your life—requires that you improvise!

Improv Is in Our Blood

We all can and do get scripted in our lives. We're creatures of habit, with routines and a host of things we regularly say and do. While you (probably) don't pick up an actual script on the way to work in the morning, it can seem like you're following one, with a variety of stage directions: *Commute to the office by your usual route, get your coffee (or tea) the way you always have it, check e-mail, avoid Leonard if at all possible*, and so on.

All these old performances weren't always old. They came from somewhere, you made them, *and you made them by improvising*. What I mean by *improvising* here is simple: Something happened in your life (a subway delay, a particularly tasty cup of tea, yet another unpleasant moment with Leonard). You perceived this event and responded to it in a way that built upon it (learned what subway exit to use for a quick transfer, wrote down the name of that tea, looked over the floor plan of the office for alternate routes to your desk). These improvised moves, and dozens if not hundreds of others, were all fresh and different...once. Then they became standard operating procedure, and after a while all these former improvisations became daily scripts.

In chapter 1, I talked about how, through improvised play and performance, children (with the unconditional support to improvise from the big people in their lives) learn how to speak and much more. When we get older (and presumably wiser), we can lose sight of the playful performances that made us wiser in the first place. Our moments of wisdom become cast in stone. From relatively inconsequential preferences such as how you like your hot beverages, to pretty important issues like your style of leadership—it's as if these once improvised performances were always there and now they define who we *really* are.

We forget that we produced and made all of this up in the first place, and that we can continue to produce who we are, what we do, how we do it, and how we feel, see, and think. So I want to reignite your ability to improvise—to make stuff up—deliberately and proactively. Not just when you're forced to by circumstances beyond your control (although that's a really good time for it); and not just when you need to come up with some new ideas (ditto), but *all the time.*

There's another reason I'm so in love with improvisation in work and life: Improvisation is a form of developmental *play* for adults. And play—which is essential to growth and learning when we're kids—can continue to help us grow and learn as adults. "Play makes people scintillate. It creates a kind of mental click that frees you to begin sorting things out. The lack of play dulls a person—and it may well be that an overall lack of play dulls a society." That was UCSF professor Lenore Terr in her book *Beyond Love and Work: Why Adults Need to Play.* Stuart Brown, the founder of the National Institute for Play, says, "Of all animal species, humans are the biggest players of all. We are built to play and built through play. When we play, we are engaged in the purest expression of our humanity."

"The rental car didn't have one."

The form of play we call improvisation is more popular than ever, both for professional actors and for nonperformers who take improv classes at schools and theaters dotting the globe. And using improvisation in business is no longer a rarity. There are hundreds, maybe thousands of people and organizations tapping into the power of this playful art form in business contexts.

Some might think this improv mania is a fad. My money is on its being around for a long time, in part because I see it as a lot more than a cool technique to help people think on their feet and be more collaborative and creative. It is all that to be sure, but improvisation is also a key part of what it means to be human. And it's essential if you want to continue to learn, grow, and develop. As the twentieth-century painter Edward Hopper said, "More of me comes out when I improvise." Improvisation is yet another way to look at *becoming* who you are not yet. When you're improvising, you can do more, see more, create more, and *be* more of who you are. You're engaged in growing and learning and doing things before you know how. As such, improvisation is one of the most effective tools for helping to enhance your performance no matter what your job is. And have I mentioned that it can improve not just your job but your entire life?

The Six Tenets of Improv

Improvisers live by a set of core tenets that guide them onstage. They're the ones Marian reminded me of earlier. And since we are all performers, we're going to focus in on these tenets as they relate to performing work and life, offstage.

Tenet #1: Yes, and...

The cardinal rule of improvisation is that no matter what's thrown at you, you always respond, "Yes, and..." Those two powerful little words are the first of our tenets, because you can't do any of the others if you're not doing this. You say yes to someone quacking like a duck (maybe by peeping like a duckling). Yes to being a surgeon whose nurse assistant has just caught you hiding the Hope Diamond in a patient's intestines (perhaps you chip off a corner of the diamond as a bribe). Yes to the performer who calls you "Daddy" in a scene set at a police station, even though you planned on playing a cop. Improvisers say yes to everything they hear and see. Then they top off their "yes" with an "and."

And is the word that leads to building on everything you hear and see, what I called "offers" in chapter 5 on listening. As I said, in everyday work and life we're presented with all kinds of offers all the time. But we don't necessarily think of them as offers. Maybe you get invited to a meeting you haven't been included in before. Or you get excluded from a meeting you think you should have been included in. Or your boss praises you in front of your co-workers. Or she cuts you off in the middle of a sentence. No matter how attractive or unattractive the offer might appear to be initially, the first step toward being able to accept it and build creatively with it is to see that it *is* an offer.

And saying yes doesn't mean you have to agree with everything you hear. Saying yes means that you're finding a way to build with another person. You're saying yes to *the person*, not necessarily to the specifics of what they said. You are opening a door to the unknown; creating a positive environment and the possibility of something brand-new. Keith Johnstone, a founding pioneer of modern improvisation, wrote, "Those that say YES are rewarded by the adventures they have. Those that say NO are rewarded by the safety they attain." *Yes*, Keith, *yes*.

"Yes, and..." in Action

In chapter 5 I introduced Sara, whom we were training to supervise inner-city teen interns at her company. Sara came into a practice role-play with a prepared list of get-to-know-you questions for D'Andre, the young man playing her intern, and the scene didn't go so well. D'Andre didn't respond the way Sara expected or wanted. But instead of listening to him and saying "Yes, and..." to his offers, she just plowed ahead with her prefabricated questions, thereby grinding their conversation to a painful halt.

After this role-play (and a few others with similar results), we knew the group needed a crash course in "Yes, and." Here's the exercise we had them do:

In groups of four people, they were the committee responsible for their ten-year high school reunion. They had an unlimited budget, access to any resources they wanted, and full authority to plan the big event. Then we told them that after the first person puts out an idea, like "Let's hold the reunion in Paris," or "Beyoncé should perform at the party," every person who speaks after that must begin their sentence with "Yes, but..."

And so they began to plan. I eavesdropped on one group:

"Yes, but Paris is too far away and no one speaks French."

"Yes, but we can have French lessons."

"Yes, but that just makes the party like school again."

Other groups were having similar results. Reunion after reunion was undermined as people negated everything with "yes, but." Everyone was frustrated. A few had stopped talking altogether.

Then came part 2. They were to do exactly the same thing—same unlimited budget, resources, and total authority—only this time, they had to start each sentence with "Yes, *and*."

Again, I listened in:

"Let's hold the reunion in Paris."

"Yes, and we can use one of the rooms in the Louvre!"

"Yes, and everyone can come as a character from a painting!"

"Yes, and we can serve wine from the vintage of each of the paintings!"

"Yes, and when we've drunk enough, we can join a secret society, hook up with Tom Hanks, and find the Holy Grail!"

Quelle difference! Now we had a bunch of cool, crazy reunion parties in the works.

We don't always have to say the actual words *Yes, and* (although it doesn't hurt, especially when you're getting started). It's more of an *activity* than a set phrase. By doing the "Yes, and" activity, Sara was able to respond completely differently to her actual intern, Lavon, who arrived a month after the training. She saw him get to the office early, identified it as an offer, and then acknowledged it and built on it by telling him it was great to keep coming in before 9 a.m. She saw that Lavon was shy, identified that as an offer, and built on it by asking him if he was nervous. He said he was, and she built on *that* offer by sharing her own nervousness when she started her first job. As a result of this and more, Lavon was able to relax a bit (and so was Sara). They could then connect and get a good start to the first day of work, Lavon's internship, Sara's tenure as a supervisor, and their relationship.

Not bad for a couple of three-letter words.

Tenet #2: Make the Other Person Look Good

Many of us go through life without giving much attention to making other people (colleagues, a boss, a subordinate, friend, family member, customer, etc.) "look good." But one of the most powerful things that improvisers do onstage to create their spontaneous "magic" is to convey with their responses that whatever their partner said or did was perfect—that it was *exactly* the right thing to say or do. It's another way of building on and with offers. The improv guru and genius Del Close captured this when he said, "If we treat each other as if we are geniuses, poets, and artists, we have a better chance of becoming that…"

The "Make the Other Person Look Good" improv tenet gives us a new performance to do at work, and we can play it any number of ways. Sometimes it can be as simple as saying, "What I really like about what Grace is saying…"; or, "Let's get back to Curtis's point, because I think it could help us think about this problem in a new way." Or publicly appreciating people who might not expect it (because they are never publicly appreciated): "I give a lot of the credit for this quarter's results to the admin team—without their support we'd all be in a lot of trouble." These are examples of "lines" to say that can help you capture an aspect of this tenet. But it's more than that. It brings us back to building ensembles everywhere. It's a "we" orientation, where you're invested not just in your own success but also in the success of others. As such, it actually redefines what success is. The improv scene succeeds when everyone looks good, and making that happen is a choice, a leadership performance.

Make the Other Person Look Good in Action

In chapter 2 we met Natasha, the accomplished executive who was performing as a leader only part-time. Natasha was often quiet and somewhat reserved, and we learned that one of her standout skills was giving concrete, on-the-ground examples of her boss's strategy and the organization's success. To up Natasha's leadership on her team, Natasha's boss, Jorge, asked Natasha to make use of her ability to connect the dots and help translate her strategic initiatives to others.

We set up a practice session with Natasha and a few of her colleagues to work on how to provide leadership by making others look good. Maureen Kelly, who was Natasha's coach, had them perform a meeting where they needed to get a new project off the ground. The rule of the exercise was that they were charged to be more appreciative of one another than usual. Natasha did a stellar job in this rehearsal by expressing her appreciation with clearly articulated examples of why what others were saying or doing was important to moving forward the project objectives—making others look good while educating them about different aspects of the project at the same time.

In the actual town hall meeting that followed, Natasha's rehearsal paid off big-time. She was able to connect her new translator character to the specific goal of focusing a spotlight on the contributions of the team to Jorge's strategic plans. Jorge, key folks on the rollout, and the team—including Natasha, of course—all looked great, because Natasha was making them shine.

Tenet #3: Celebrate Mistakes and Failures

Mistakes can be the bane of our existence, no matter where we are in the occupational food chain. We waste so much energy trying to hide them, deflect blame for them, or defend ourselves from blame. And we just plain feel bad—humiliated, embarrassed, angry—about our own mistakes and the mistakes of others.

"We stigmatize mistakes," says Sir Ken Robinson (of whom I'm a big fan, along with the more than thirty-six million viewers of his 2006 TED talk). He continues: "And we're now running national educational systems where mistakes are the worst thing you can make. And the result is that we are educating people out of their creative capacities."

Let's stop stigmatizing mistakes and crushing people's creative capacities. The question is: How? What do we do with those mistakes, and how do we relate to the people (you know, the human beings) who make them in a way that's productive and not destructive?

If we look to improvisation, the answer is nothing short of reveling in them. The best onstage improvisers know that audiences delight in mistakes and love to watch someone deal with them in a playful, refreshing, and honest way. The very night I told you about at the beginning of this chapter, it happened to Marian. She walked into a scene with a character who, in an earlier scene, had been named Don. But in this scene, she called him Dean. Instead of correcting her, or pretending she had said the right name, or any of the "normal" ways of responding to mistakes, her scene partner didn't drop a beat. "You seem to have me confused with my evil twin," he said. The audience went crazy, the scene went on, and we now had the central plot device that fueled the rest of the show.

Improvisers and audiences alike breathe a collective sigh of relief when mistakes are creatively played with. Allowing for and even celebrating mistakes can help create an environment that produces trust, experimentation, and risk-taking—those essential building blocks for growth and new learning, as well as innovation and creativity. I'm not saying it's easy. Case in point: About ten years ago, I made a mistake that cost POAL hundreds of thousands of dollars when we were a young company without that kind of money to lose. I had been interviewed by one of the biggest print publications in the world, and I made a serious faux pas by speaking a little too unguardedly about one of POAL's clients...on the front page, no less. The coverage was excellent. The response from the client I had named? We were not so much fired as *banned*. To this day.

Celebrate? Hardly. If I was going to do anything with a bottle of champagne that day, it would have been to hit myself over the head with it. I remember talking with Fred Newman, my mentor and a co-founder of POAL. In tears, I told him this sordid story. He was silent for a long moment.

Then Fred said to me, "Congratulations, Cathy."

Wait. What?

"This is an excellent mistake," he said. "It's really good. You don't get to make mistakes like this unless you're in the big leagues. So congratulations!"

Wow, I never would have thought of it that way, that's for sure. I was busy wallowing in my mortification and regret. But it was true. I was able see the mistake for what it was: (1) It was *huge*; (2) it was an indicator of the success of our fledgling firm; and (3) it was the most efficient media training class ever. Not to mention a crash course in how to think about and learn from mistakes.

And no, I'm not going to tell you the name of the client. Some mistakes you celebrate only once.

Celebrate Mistakes and Failures in Action

In chapter 6 I introduced you to Colin, the CEO of the design and consulting firm where genius but total-pain-in-the-butt Marcus was making life miserable. But as problematic as Marcus's behavior was, Colin and his team had contributed to the toxic office environment by letting it go on largely unchallenged and unchecked. Major managerial mistake. And we were able to help Marcus explore the multiple mistakes that he was making as well, from the incompetent to the negligent, that together produced the load of crap that everyone else was suffering through. What were they able to ultimately do with all of these "mistakes"? Play with them, celebrate them, and create with them.

As a way to help people start doing something different with mistakes, the first thing we do is get them to make some. We put them in standing circles of about ten people and give them ninety seconds to memorize one another's names (or if they know one another, their middle names or made-up superhero names). The game itself consists of taking turns pointing to people around the circle and accurately saying their names. Of course, with ninety seconds to prepare, they make mistakes, and when that happens, the fun begins. The person who got it wrong throws his or her arms up in the air and proudly exclaims, "I made a mistake!" and takes a bow as the circle breaks into thunderous applause.

Then that participant leaves to join another circle (where, of course, they don't know anybody's name).

It's a silly and energizing exercise. People laugh, cheer, run around, breathe hard, and laugh some more. And they also scratch their heads (literally and figuratively) when, later, we begin to unpack what we just did and why:

"It was so counterintuitive and weird to get applause for a mistake, and to be actually proud of it. It turns that whole idea upside down."

"What a different way to relate to mistakes. So refreshing."

"This is all well and good for certain mistakes...but not stupid ones or ones that people keep making."

"Wow. Not sure we could pull off this kind of positive attitude around here."

This exercise is meant to sort of shock people (in a friendly, funny way) into reconsidering how we relate to mistakes. As you can see, the conversation produces a bit of soul-searching and some *ahas* about the current plays people are in (both individually and organizationally) and how we relate to learning and growing from mistakes. When it comes to our performances around mistakes, even moving the needle just a little bit can be big. Am I advocating for people to make mistakes? Nope. I don't have to—because we all make them. What I'm advocating for is what happens next. Even when "learning from failure" is part of an organization's values, at the end of the day other rules clearly apply. There may be learning, sure, but there's also plenty of fear, shame, butt-covering, and finger-pointing that keep that learning to a minimum.

So let's push beyond the slogans about learning from our mistakes. Even if it's just a little bit, start performing a different culture of mistake-making. Sometimes this means talking about your mistake with someone you trust to help you unpack what you can learn from it. Sometimes it can mean whooping, hollering, clapping, and bowing as a way to break the pattern of blame. Either way, you can get on the road to discovering the real growth that can come from mistakes—yours, mine, and others'.

Tenet #4: Follow the Follower

After every performance my improv group does, we have a tradition of gathering outside the theater and greeting the audience. We chat, talk about the show, and sign autographs. And when the show has been par-ticularly good, somebody—often several people—pulls one of us aside and says, "Okay. Level with me. How much of that was scripted? Because you can't have just made it all up." It's fun when that happens, because the answer is always the same—*none* of it was scripted; *all* of it emerged in the moment. But to our audience, it looks like magic. And how that "magic" happens brings me to our next tenet: Follow the Follower.

Viola Spolin, considered by many to be the originator of modern improvisation, first described the phenomenon of "following the follower" in her seminal work on improvisation for actors in the 1960s. In the con-text of business, it's a heightening and extending of the "Yes, and" concept to include how to think about leadership and, perhaps more important, how to lead. Typically, at work you're either leading *or* following. But when you're performing—improvising your way through your workaday scenes as the leader of a team or its most junior member—there's actually a simultaneous *I'm following you while you're following me* happening. When you're following the follower on the job, just like on the improv stage, there is a seamless give-and-take, a creative "making it up together" going on.

Follow the Follower in Action

In chapter 2 I introduced you to Carter and Franz, who worked at an ad agency. Project manager Franz reported to creative director Carter, and both of them dreaded their weekly catch-up meetings. Carter felt they were a big waste of time. Franz got that message loud and clear, but he really needed these meetings to move projects along and effectively do his job. Indeed, nothing much was getting produced except frustration.

One of the first things we had Carter and Franz do together was the "mirroring" exercise. If you recall from the prologue of this book, this silent exercise starts with a pair facing each other. Slowly, one person (the "leader") begins to move, and the other person (the "follower") mirrors that movement at exactly the same time. After a little while, we instruct the leader and the follower to switch roles without abruptly changing whatever movement they're doing. Later in the exercise, the pairs are told that there is no leader, and the performers simply reflect each other's movements. In other words, they are literally following the follower. It's mesmerizing to do and to watch as the two participants seem to become one organism.

As out of sync as Carter and Franz were, it was particularly rewarding to watch them do the mirror exercise together. At first, they had trouble even looking at each other, let alone moving in unison. But after a couple of minutes, it looked like they had been doing this for years.

In our discussion following the exercise, Carter had a realization: The hierarchy between him and Franz had become an impediment to their relationship. Carter had stopped thinking they were working together and simply saw Franz as working *for* him. So when Franz was, for example, "taking too long" to understand an issue, or (worse, in Carter's view) offering his own opinion or point of view about how to proceed, Carter thought it was just a waste of time. But the mirroring exercise helped Carter to see that, hierarchy aside, he and Franz were actually working *together.* Yes, he was the leader, but every move he made produced a resulting move from Franz. And when he ignored or failed to adjust to Franz's moves, the two of them either stalled or created friction. Seen in this light, Franz's contributions (even his difficulty comprehending the intricacies of Carter's explanations) became creative challenges that engaged Carter. Franz then felt appreciated for all the hard work he was doing, which made it easier to accept all the offers, good and bad, that Carter was giving him.

Tenet # 5: Delight in Curveballs

If you always know what's going to happen next, you're either bored, boring, or the Amazing Kreskin. Curveballs are a part of life, and the workplace is filled with them. They can be small, like being asked to speak in a meeting about something that wasn't on the agenda. They can be huge, like when your debut product that was supposed to hit the shelves in April won't be arriving until July. Or anywhere in between. Regardless of size, curveballs are a regular part of our days. And left to our own devices, we tend to fear them, get rattled, and try to run for the hills when they arrive.

But improvisers *love* curveballs (and lest we forget, you are an improviser). Their very unexpectedness raises your game. You have to listen harder and use more creativity and imagination in your responses. Curveballs change the trajectory of a scene and lead you to places you hadn't planned to go. Getting better at fielding them makes you more resilient and effective.

And so, curveballs are really just offers—small offers or big fat juicy offers—that you didn't see coming. You can delight in them. Be creative with them. Wildly, brilliantly creative? Maybe. But more often, a bit more mundane. Sort of like, "Oh! What happens next?" and you're one of the people who get to create an answer to that question.

Delight in Curveballs in Action

In chapter 3 I introduced you to my old friend Jenna, a national organizer for an environmental organization. She was complaining to a bunch of friends and colleagues about how underappreciated she was at work, despite her tenure and accomplishments. We'd heard the same sad story many times before and were all more than a little bored by it. Jenna desperately needed something to get her out of her loop of negativity. Kishanda led the way. Instead of doing the usual I'm-so-sorry-this-is-happening-to-you script, she came out and told Jenna just what a piece of work she was. Curveball!

We have an exercise that helps our clients to play with curveballs. It goes like this: People get into pairs (Persons A and B) and face each other. Person A can see a screen or TV monitor; Person B can't. Person A gets a topic to speak about to Person B (the latest reorganization at work, the first-quarter results, how to be more customer-focused, etc.). Soon after Person A starts talking, a random word or phrase appears on the screen (e.g., *lawn mower*). Now Person A has to incorporate this word—this curveball—into their monologue seamlessly, as if it were exactly what they would have said anyway. On the screen, the curveballs keep coming: "car trouble," "Kim Kardashian," "salt," and so on, and Person A has to incorporate each one. It's a real brain-stretcher, and people amaze themselves and one another with how creative and inventive they can be.

Dealing with curveballs in this way is like a muscle that starts out puny but is actually pretty easy to build. Many of us are so afraid we won't be able to handle curveballs that we try to avoid them completely. But if we work that muscle, both intellectually and emotionally, we can handle more than we realize. Kishanda's curveball left Jenna way off balance—shocked, confused, and infuriated (which is a pretty common emotional combination when you're dealing with the unexpected). But when Jenna let the curveball take her to a different way of understanding her character and the play she was in, it made a lot less sense to make the same old choices. The result was that she was able to make a bunch of new choices, which made being at work a lot more tolerable.

Same old, same old is almost never something to celebrate. And since life likes to toss lots of curveballs our way, it's helpful to know how to play with—or even better, delight in—the ones that cross your plate.

Tenet # 6: Go into the Cave

I'm ending with the scariest tenet. This tenet asks the improviser to be willing to go anywhere, follow his or her fear, and go deep into...*the cave!!!* (Cue scary music.) "Entering the cave" goes something like this: You find yourself in a scene/relationship where, in response to an offer from your scene partner, you have a choice to make. You can respond in a way that's predictable or comfortable because you've done it before and have a pretty good idea how it's going to go, *or* respond by saying or doing something outside your usual repertoire, where you and others can't predict what'll happen and where you know you're taking a risk.

At work there's plenty that's superficial, and, a lot of the time, that's just fine. When you walk into the office, you don't have to hug the receptionist. Or if you are the receptionist, you don't have to ask people how they are and then insist that they *really* tell you how they are. But there are also plenty of situations where taking certain kinds of risks—asking different kinds of questions, having conversations that are hard, doing something for the first time that will most likely fail—is *exactly* what's needed. Your ability to inspire and motivate others when the stakes are high and risks are great may depend on the example you set, and that's when it's time to go into the cave.

Go into the Cave in Action

I've told you about our signature exercise, the One-Minute Performance of a Lifetime, and it's often an experience of going into the cave. One such performance came from Ryan, a longtime client and the head of HR at a manufacturing firm. We were working with an international cohort of their senior execs, focusing on expanding their performance in handling ambiguity and change.

In his minute, Ryan showed us a conversation with his dad, a decorated World War II veteran, whom he referred to as "the Colonel." The Colonel was in assisted living, and on this particular day Ryan had brought him books and movies and was helping to feed him. He spoke gently to the Colonel, telling him that no, his wife's name was not Mary, it was Maria; and that no, Mom and Diana couldn't have visited with him earlier; they hadn't come to the home.

After one minute I called "Curtain," and, as expected, Ryan received a huge round of applause. For his sequel, I directed Ryan to play the role of the Colonel, and to let "Ryan" (played by me) know that he appreciated how Ryan had taken care of him.

I saw him hesitate. I was inviting Ryan further into the cave with me, and he seemed unsure if he could do it. Then he sat down in a chair and closed his eyes. The scene began, and as "Ryan," I sat silently, and he opened his eyes. I listened to "the Colonel" speak haltingly in a monotone. "Thank you, son. I know this must have been hard for you. You think that I didn't see you, or hear you, or know you much of the time. But I did. Every time you came, I knew it was you, I just couldn't speak the words." As "Ryan," I sat still and nodded and held "my father's" hand. Then the scene ended and his colleagues gave Ryan a standing ovation. I was deeply moved to have been part of that moment with him.

The following week, I received an e-mail from Ryan:

Cathy—

On behalf of our organization, I really wanted to thank you for your outstanding work with us this past week. It was hard but extremely valuable and I am so glad that we had the opportunity to work with you.

On a personal note, I also wanted to tell you a little more about the performance you helped me to give. You see, my mother and sister were passengers on American Airlines Flight 11, the first plane flown into the World Trade Center. It was a horrific time to be sure for everyone but especially for my father, the Colonel, who lost his wife of 51 years and his only daughter. It was too much for him to handle and we believe triggered him into Alzheimer's disease. We ended up putting him into an assisted-care facility where he lived until he died in 2006. I tried my best to take care of him and my family while doing a high-stress job at work, and it was very painful for me to see him decline both mentally and physically. But it was also a blessing to have him with us.

So, when I performed this as part of our workshop, it was incredibly emotional for me but also therapeutic as well. When you asked me to perform as my father I didn't think I could do it. It made me feel how lonely he was and how afraid he must have been. It also made me feel good that he knew deep inside that he was grateful that I was there for him. Thank you for doing this for me—it was hard, but extremely valuable. For the first time since 9/11, I have been able to really feel that I could get all of these emotions off my chest, and the connection this has allowed with my colleagues has had a profound impact on our abilities to work together.

Kind Regards and Best Wishes,

Ryan

You can imagine how I felt when I read Ryan's note. It was a risk for Ryan to perform this story with his colleagues back then, and to share more with me through this note. When you go into the cave, you can't control or plan. It can be, as Ryan said, "hard but extremely valuable." You can go places that are important, interesting, meaningful, and unexpected. As a leader, it means opening up in new, authentic, and creative ways. Performing your life—improvising in this way with others—creates the possibility of going places that are unknown and unknowable. You become more engaged because you're doing something with and for others that doesn't come easy. The rest of us become more engaged because we're seeing you in a new way, and that impacts not only who you are—but who they are.

Make Up Your Own Improvisation Tenets...Continuously

Following most of our programs with clients, we give participants a tip card with a set of suggestions and directions for new performances to try going forward. Consider the tenets of improv that I've just shared as this book's tip card...with one important addition: *Make up your own tenets.* That's what improvisation is all about, after all.

Improvise Your Life Exercises

1. Say **"Yes, and"** for an entire week at work and at home. Even if you don't say the words, listen carefully to what you hear (and see). Then, whatever you've perceived, say yes to it, and then add something that accepts and builds with it. After you do this for a week, continue doing it for the rest of your life.

2. **Make 'em look good:** Help somebody out with a piece of work so that (1) she learns something; (2) the work gets better; and (3) she gets the credit. And for a bonus (not for you, but for someone else), in a meeting or two, respond to what someone says with the starting phrase "What I really like about what you said..."

3. Tell some colleagues about a doozy of a **mistake** you've made—today, yesterday, this year, in your life. Or open a meeting with it. Tell them you'd like them to applaud once they hear your mistake, and then you take a bow. Ask people for their thoughts about what you and the organization might do to grow and learn from your mistake. Come up with real, specific ideas about this—not generalizations.

4. **Follow the follower:** Listen, respond, and follow someone (i.e., let him lead you) in a conversation, idea, or process when you might not typically do that. Let what he says and does affect what you say and do. See where you end up and what the experience of doing so is like.

5. Throw yourself a few **curveballs**. Make a decision without thinking it through carefully and thoroughly. Talk to someone at work you never talk with. Talk to a stranger and get into a philosophical conversation. When someone says or does something at work that throws you off balance, notice it. Smile and breathe. "Yes-and" it.

6. **Go into the cave:** Bring up an "elephant in the room" in a positive way. Ask someone about something personal that you know about but haven't really talked about. (Use your judgment about what's appropriate, of course.)

ACT III

CREATE YOUR NEW PLAY

*How to Perform and Improvise
the Daily Scenes of Your Life*

INTRODUCTION TO ACT III

Make believe you're brave
And the trick will take you far.
You may be as brave
As you make believe you are.

—*From* The King and I
by Rodgers and Hammerstein

By now you've met, in detail, some of the leaders and business professionals my team and I have worked with over the past twenty years. I've talked about how we've directed them, the new performances they've tried, and how this has changed them personally and professionally, transforming their teams, their colleagues, and their organizations.

I've also shared with you performance exercises for everyday work that are about stretching and growing in small and big ways. I hope you've been trying them and having some performance breakthroughs as a result. I urge you to keep going back to these exercises and also to modify them as you see fit. You know by now that the POAL approach is not linear or step-by-step, so my direction to you is to keep your creative juices flowing as you perform in new and varied ways.

In Act III, I want to continue this process by giving you some new tools and exercises to further develop your performance muscles, mindset, and moxie. A note about exercises and tools: We usually think of a tool as a specific means to produce a specific result. If you need to get a nail into a wall, you grab a hammer. If you want to fix your favorite ceramic mug, you get some glue and start piecing it back together. Following that model, if you want to become a better storyteller or influencer, you find an exercise or a tool to address that issue. And I'll be giving you some of those in the pages that follow.

But that's not the whole picture. It simply is not the case that the kind of learning and growth we're going for here comes from implementing a cool technique or two. Think about it this way: When you go to the gym and work hard on your arms and abs, you can get buff and produce an awesome six-pack. But you're also doing more. You're getting stronger. You're becoming healthier. You're more in touch with your body and expanding what it can do (while learning what it can't). As a result, you can do new exercises and moves that you might never have imagined possible. You use your body and muscles in new ways.

Performance tools are like exercise. They don't produce just one result. They're like working out at a kind of growth-and-development gym. In addition to helping you solve a problem or meet a challenge, they help you to keep developing your creative capacity to improvise, grow, and create change. As your performance muscles grow, you'll create new tools in an ever-expanding learning and development cycle.

Pretending Your Way to Authenticity

It would be a misstep for me to now move directly onto these tools without talking about the A-word. I learned that lesson early on in our workshops and trainings. It's inevitable that when I direct you to perform being generous with someone you feel intimidated by, or suggest an out-of-character opening line for a challenging conversation, or ask you to perform an operatic version of your Monday morning meeting, you may feel like I'm telling you to abandon your *authenticity*. This comes up all the time in every kind of training that we do. So let me take a moment to address it head-on.

Herminia Ibarra says, "We tend to latch on to authenticity as an excuse for sticking with what's comfortable. But few jobs allow us to do that for long. That's doubly true when we advance in our careers or when demands or expectations change...Career advances require all of us to move way beyond our comfort zones."

So, imagine you're at a family wedding, stuck in a corner and a conversation with your eighty-one-year-old uncle Artie, the retired plumbing contractor. (If you don't have an eighty-one-year-old retired plumbing contractor for an uncle, feel free to use mine—he'll talk to anybody.) It's one of those conversations (far from the first) in which Artie is going on and on about the perils of non-PVC pipes. I give you a direction: to perform as an interested and curious listener, even though it's the last thing on earth you want to do. While it may seem that I'm asking you to be inauthentic—to negate how you really feel—I'm not. I'm directing you to access different parts of who you are; to tap into your ability to improvise, explore, challenge, play with, and be creative with a situation, person, or relationship at the very same time as you're (perhaps justifiably) bored out of your skull. Sure, you can continue to play the scene the way you always do (thinly veiled loathing). The play will go on, and Artie won't get any more interesting.

But if you access other parts of yourself, more of yourself, and perform curiosity and interest, here's some of what could happen: You now have something new to do while he drones on, making the situation less boring. You hear offers and find something in what he said that you *can* build with, which actually makes the conversation more productive and interesting. You learn something about him and his work that you never knew before. You show other people in the family how to effectively handle this guy (it's a leadership performance!). All while continuing to build your performance and improvisational muscles. And your uncle— who's been talking nonstop on this topic for sixty years and hasn't seen anyone actually look interested for the past fifty-four—is going to have a very different kind of experience in this conversation. Who knows what *he'll* do in return.

As you can see, I'm calling into question what people usually mean by "the one, real, true me." I want to challenge what most people mean when they say they need to be their *authentic* selves. If that means holding on to some single version of themselves, or only expressing their "loudest" feeling or their initial reaction(s), they're leaving a hell of a lot out. They're leaving out their authentic *multiplicity*.

Vera and Theo, the senior director/project management team at the software company we met in chapter 5, were performing their disagreement in ways that were destructive but felt authentic to them. When they made the performance explicit by portraying each other, they discovered they had a multiplicity of performance choices that were far more productive and arguably *more* authentic, since they gave expression to their real and shared commitment to their project, their company, and their client.

Nicholas (in chapter 2) performed as Scott, the Super Salesman, in order to expand who he was and how he expressed himself. He never stopped being Nicholas by doing that. He was able to access a unique and authentic human ability to perform in different ways, and by doing so he discovered and tapped into parts of himself that sticking with his "real me" wouldn't have allowed. More multiplicity.

And Alicia, who tried a new performance with her perpetually tardy husband by dancing with him instead of fighting with him, was not denying the essence of her feelings of neglect and annoyance. She made a choice to draw upon a couple of other things she authentically likes to do (dance, love the guy) and performed that version of herself the next time he came home late. By performing this way she discovered that she's an innovator of sorts who could take a highly unpleasant situation and make it downright fun.

All these business professionals released themselves from the idea that the ways they felt at any given moment were their true, authentic feelings, which somehow had to be preserved and honored lest they violate their true selves. They let go of the notion of their "essence" or "core" and *performed themselves* in new ways, so that they and others could access the multiplicity and complexity of who they are. "Do I contradict myself?" Walt Whitman wrote. "Very well then I contradict myself. (I am large, I contain multitudes.)" Indeed. To be authentic means to access and embrace our contradictions and the multitudes we contain. Our multiplicity is, after all, essential to being human. In describing what is unique about human beings, Fred Newman wrote in his book *Let's Develop!* that we "create and re-create our lives even as we are living them. Are we shaped by our biology? No question about it: we are without wings, and so we're unable to fly on our own. Are we formed by society? Clearly: the language we speak, at least at first, is our 'mother tongue.' But we are unlike any other species in that we have the capacity to choose, to organize and reorganize culture—to alter the experience of experience itself. No other species, so far as anyone can tell, can do this."

So while hedgehogs and ants and monkeys certainly may change and be changed by things, they can't change through their own conscious activity. They can't choose to live their lives in different ways. Human beings can, and do, and to be truly authentic is to exercise this ability. Our authenticity lives in the growth space of being both who we are and who we are not, at the same time.

"*The cocoon, the braces, the acne—I don't miss that phase of my life at all.*"

The Scenes of Our Lives

At POAL we help people to meet the challenges in the life cycle of their careers—from leaders at the top of their game to leaders-in-the-making. Using the Becoming Principle, we focus on the most prevalent themes in their lives to accelerate their continuous learning and developing. Those themes? Sales and networking; coaching and mentoring others; handling challenging conversations; presence; storytelling. Within and around all of these themes we are strengthening relationships; motivating and inspiring people; influencing without authority; leading with authenticity; working and playing with creativity; innovating. In Act III we'll go into greater depth on these scenes and themes, and you'll get techniques and tools for working on them. The exercise section of each chapter is designed to fit the specific challenges at hand while building on the performance ideas and tools in Acts I and II, and always in the service of creating new and breakthrough performances—of you.

and then... and then...

We're All Storytellers

> "I could tell you my adventures—beginning from this morning," said Alice a little timidly: "but it's no use going back to yesterday, because I was a different person then."
>
> "Explain all that," said the Mock Turtle.
>
> "No, no! the adventures first," said the Gryphon in an impatient tone: "explanations take such a dreadful time."
>
> —*Lewis Carroll*, Alice's Adventures in Wonderland

Meet Ogg the caveman. One day he goes out to hunt and spends three hours trekking to the watering hole of the dik-diks, a tiny antelope breed. Ogg waits ten hours, sitting in one spot waiting for the dik-diks to arrive. The dik-diks finally come. Ogg kills a dik-dik. Ogg does his three-hour trek home. Pretty dull story, right?

Now imagine Ogg reenacting it for his wife, Ugga. He pants as he recounts the hike to the watering hole, using his handmade spear as a cane, and making sure to point out landmarks Ugga will remember from their last vacation in the area. Crouching behind the stone that serves as an ottoman in the living-room space of their cave, Ogg shows her his hiding place…and waits. Seconds pass, and Ugga is on the edge of her rock. He imitates the tentative, tasty, and delicate dik-dik as it enters the valley. He makes the sound of a crunching leaf and jolts his head forward. Then he dramatically raises his spear high into the air…and stops. Ugga draws in a breath. Ogg turns to her, his face a perfect imitation of the innocent, fawn-like dik-dik. His features become a mask of his own sadness as he contemplates ending this innocent life, then contort in a spasm of hunger as the possible consequence of letting it go sinks in. Then back to sadness, then hunger; a perfect depiction of his inner turmoil. Tears well up in

Ugga's eyes. Suddenly, Ogg turns his head as if listening to a far-off sound, and from his throat comes an imitation of a baby crying. His eyes meet Ugga's, and her hand moves involuntarily to her abdomen, where, indeed, their soon-to-be cave-baby resides. Ogg's face turns to steely resolve, and he thrusts his spear into the heart of the animal. He lets loose a scream—half victory, half regret—and Ugga laughs through her tears.

The next day, determined that her husband should never again face such a dilemma, Ugga goes out into the forest in the back of the cave and invents farming.

The facts of Ogg's hunting trip are simple. Ogg's telling of the story is not, and the impact of his performance—vivid, personal, dramatic, and emotional—is significant. Ugga comes to know her husband better through the telling, he comes to know her and himself better, and their relationship is enhanced and solidified. Not to mention that it precipitates a change in the course of human history.

Performing Stories

Unless you're a professional actor or an amateur clown, chances are when you have a story to tell, you do it as your "normal" self. Which can be a fine way to tell a good story. But the telling is within the confines of who you are, and if you've been paying attention, you know I think that kind of self-definition can be a big limitation. So I'd like to take you on a bit of a hike of your own in this chapter, to the watering hole of the Becoming Principle (I know, the metaphor is a stretch here), where you can try out some new performances of you as a storyteller. Because when you *perform* a story, a world of choices and new possibilities opens up. Sometimes it's a small but high-impact performance choice that helps you to create and express a story in a way that is more personal, funny, or candid. Sometimes the act of creating/discovering/telling a story enables you to break away from how you (the storyteller) see things. You thought the story was simply a, then b, then c. But performing as a storyteller can lead you to discover a whole new story that you hadn't told, conceived of, or understood.

And there are bigger and more dramatic choices—instead of just being you, you can be *anyone* (or *anything*—think Ogg impersonating the tiny, tasty dik-dik). Instead of just sitting in your chair, you can get up and use your body (as Ogg did when he dramatized his long hike and his kill). Instead of speaking in your normal talking voice, you can get loud...and then soft (pant or scream). You can stop time, or speed ahead, or jump around in time altogether. You can show how you feel, provide color and details that connect with your audience, and transport them to a new place, with you. You can be brave and convey something personal and meaningful to you. Some of this might sound extreme; some might be obvious. But if I can help you to expand your options and grow as a performer of stories, (a) you might never do a boring or dry presentation again; (b) you'll help people to think and feel in new ways; and (c) you'll stretch and grow yourself in the process.

Besides, storytelling itself has become big business. What's the story of your brand? How are you going to tell the story of a product? What's your company story? Every day, companies call in experts in these kinds of story-related explorations to help turn facts into something people can not just remember but also feel excited about. There's an enormous amount of good stuff out there on the craft of storytelling, so I'm going to leave most of that to the recommended reading list in the back of this book. Instead, I'll be focusing on storytelling as a *performance*. Performance is where the interplay of the *content* of a story and the *telling* of a story happens, and it can produce magic. We'll work on how and why performing stories can help your audience feel and think in new ways, and how tapping into your human ability to perform as a storyteller can be an important part of your own growth and development.

"Coming Out" Stories

When I met Charlotte, she was the COO of a large information systems company, one of only two women on the executive team. She was a formidable presence—a whip-smart, impeccably groomed woman in her late forties with a powerful command of the space around her. The company had recently made a large acquisition and as a result was going through a significant culture change. Charlotte had been brought in about a year earlier to help lead that charge, and in that time had garnered enormous respect. The CEO and the rest of the executive team had great confidence in her. But one level down in the hierarchy it was a different picture, and this was where she had asked for my help. With her tough, take-no-prisoners style, and having been (erroneously) associated with a large layoff that had occurred before she joined, Charlotte was not well liked or trusted by the very leaders whose support would make or break her ambitious plans.

I told Charlotte that if she wanted to get people to care about the issues at hand, she first had to get them to care about *her*. Her response was something along the lines of "Well, that's not going to happen. What else do you have?" Charlotte was a guarded person. When she talked, her performance was to be in control, always strong, always quick and tough. I knew that to get people to care, she was going to have to create a new performance and release some of that control; let people over the wall she had built.

Charlotte and I had been working together for a few weeks when I told her I wanted to learn more about her history, her personal story. "What makes you who you are?" I asked. "What can you share with me that nobody knows about you?"

I was taken a bit by surprise when her eyes welled up. She looked out her office window for a long moment and then took a deep breath. "Okay. Wow. Here goes," she said.

Two years earlier, Charlotte's fifteen-year marriage had ended in divorce. At work, she told no one. At around the same time, her closest friend had passed away after a long battle with cancer. She told no one. Her mother died in a car accident when Charlotte was fifteen, and soon after, her father abandoned her and her brother. Nobody knew. Charlotte quit school and worked two jobs to take care of her older brother, who years later was diagnosed as bipolar. She had a son when she was still a teenager whom she was forced to give up for adoption. Nobody knew. Eventually getting into college, Charlotte worked her butt off to be an A student while taking care of her brother for more than six years. Nobody knew. She was driven to leave her painful history behind and rise above it. And nobody knew any of it.

As I listened to Charlotte, I was spellbound. My heart ached as this accomplished woman shared her painful past. I thanked her for being so open with me, but I felt strongly that it had to be more than just me. "You need to share this story, Charlotte," I said. "You're trying to motivate your people to embrace and navigate a big change here at your company. You want to get them out of their comfort zones, take more risks, go into uncharted territory...and you are the poster child for all of that!"

Charlotte was no longer meeting my eyes, but I pushed on. "Right now, you make everything look easy. No one can relate to that. I couldn't. People think you don't know anything about struggle. But boy, are they wrong. Nothing was easy for you. Nothing! You need to share your story and let people hear that you know something up close and personal about having to change course when it's the last thing you want—and presumably are able—to do." I was practically standing on Charlotte's desk shouting at the top of my lungs.

Charlotte finally looked at me. She told me she was sure that if she shared any of this history, her colleagues would judge her, reject her, talk behind her back, and think she was crazy. And that if she tried to tell any of this story publicly, she'd "lose it," fall apart, reveal herself as "too emotional" and "just like a woman"—and not the tough, high-powered leader that she'd worked her ass off to be. "I can't do it, Cathy," she cried. "They'll crucify me."

"Yes, you can," I said, both of us crying now. "I'll help you. I'm going to help you perform your story. And even if you do fall apart onstage—which you won't—they won't crucify you. They will follow you."

Charlotte was silent again. She dabbed her eyes with a tissue and straightened a pile of papers on the table. Finally, she said, "I'll think about it. I'll get back to you."

Two weeks went by. I sent her a note to check in. Then another week. Had I pushed her too hard? And then, finally, she e-mailed me. I waited until I was home with a drink in my hand and a cat on my lap before I read it.

Dear Cathy—

I want to thank you for all the work you've done with me up to this point, and especially for your passion and commitment in working with me on my "story" last month.

"Oh, no," I said to the cat. "This is it." The note went on:

I didn't realize it at the time, but you remind me of someone.

Who—Dr. Phil? Attila the Hun? My mind raced. The cat jumped down, evidently nervous about the growling I was doing deep in my throat.

I had a boss once, early in my career. Her name was Barbara, and she was a pit bull...

"Oh, great," I said aloud, and the cat whined. "Otis, shush!" I hissed. "Let her finish."

...she was a pit bull, both as a manager, and as a person. Of all the people I've worked with before or since, she got to know me the best—she took it as her own personal challenge to do that. She shared her story with me, and wouldn't let up until I reciprocated. So I did, and so Barbara knew my story, pretty much all of it. She knew what made me tick, what drove me. And over the course of our work together, she used what she knew to push me in directions I needed to go; to motivate me and mentor me and guide me in ways she never could have otherwise.

That kind of engagement and connection is a big part of what's missing here. I want the whole company to have some of the experience I had with Barbara. You helped me to see that for that to happen, I'm going to have to make the first move. And the timing is right—I have a presentation in front of 400 of my leaders in two months.

Let's get started.

Woo-hoo! I did a little happy dance—we were going to get to create a new story! The cat rolled onto his back for a belly rub.

And so the rehearsals began. We spent the next few months crafting, improvising, writing, and rewriting both the content and the performance of her story. This was one of those life situations in which stretching and performing in a whole new way is required. Charlotte struggled with the reality of this new performance, unsure whether she could share the unshareable. As her coach, I did my best to continue to push her and challenge her.

There was no way she was going to perform this story without being emotional, so Charlotte and I worked together to discover how much she could share; what mattered most to her and what her audience would care about; when to go slow, speed up, or solicit a response; and how to craft the story so that it connected to the strategy of the organization.

And through it all, how to let people know that opening up in this way was a choice she was making—a very difficult one—to help them take on new challenges. For me personally, it was some of the most intimate directing and coaching I had ever done.

Finally, it was the day of the big speech. And while I was excited for her, I was relaxed as could be. I know, easy for me to say—I wasn't giving the talk. But here's my point: Charlotte had grown so much in this process. Creating the performance of her story was creating a new performance of herself. Telling that story now to her colleagues was just a moment in that journey. She was going to kick butt.

Later that night I got her voice mail. "I was more scared than even I thought I'd be. But I felt like I was having an intimate conversation with four hundred people. That's crazy, right? Cathy, I got a three-minute standing ovation at the end. I'm overwhelmed. Just overwhelmed."

In response to her presentation, she received dozens of e-mails, texts, and phone calls from people who had attended her presentation thanking her for her candor and inspiration, expressing their support for her initiative and—in several cases—admitting that they had gotten her all wrong up to that point.

Charlotte and I have stayed in touch since her "coming out." The change campaign she was leading has resulted in a successful postacquisition integration. Two years since she first gave that talk, all indications are for continued growth going forward.

In order to help her company to grow, Charlotte needed to grow. She had to perform who she was not—*opening up to people in this way*—in order to perform who she was; specifically, to create *more* of who she was. Performing her story did that for her and her organization.

A Bloke's Tale

Calvert had moved to New York City from London ten years ago and was now an executive vice president at an electronics manufacturer. We were leading a presentation training class with him and a half dozen other execs, and with his charming speaking voice (we Americans can be suckers for an English accent), I thought he'd be a fascinating raconteur.

In the moments before class, Calvert had shared with me the reason he was eager to work on his presentation skills: He'd been given the opening slot in a quarterly all-hands meeting, in which he was slated to unveil the amazing results of a two-year project he'd led to reverse the company's less-than-optimal environmental record.

After our warm-up exercises, I asked Calvert to get up in front of the group and tell a quick story about his work. He stood at the head of the conference room table, clasped his hands in a prayerful pose, and began speaking in a dull monotone. Three minutes later the rest of the group was yawning, checking their phones, or staring off into the middle distance. I would have said something, but I hadn't noticed because I was beginning to doze. That had never happened before, in all my years of coaching, and—with Calvert's big presentation less than a week away—I knew that he and I had a challenge on our hands.

"Do other dads always read bedtime PowerPoints?"

Calvert didn't need to share his personal history with his audience as Charlotte had. But he did need to do more than educate them about brominated flame retardants (BFRs). He needed to get them excited, inspired, and to feel some of the justified pride he felt at helping the company achieve a twelve-spot jump in a highly publicized "green electronics" ranking. So after he finished telling the story in front of the group (and after giving the group a break to go get coffee and splash ice water on their faces), I asked Calvert how he felt when he got the news of the results.

"I was gobsmacked," he said. After a brief, confused discussion of what that meant (it's British for "astonished to the point of near unconsciousness"), we continued.

"If you had wanted to share exactly how you felt at that moment," I asked, "and you could talk to anyone you wanted, anywhere in the world, what would you have done?"

A faraway look came into Calvert's eyes. "I'd have met up with my old mates from [here he named his former company, a UK-based competitor] at the pub across the street from the office. Those wankers think they take the biscuit for being green, but we've made mincemeat of them this year."

"What do those wankers call you?"

Calvert smiled. "Richard. From when I worked in cellular handsets." My blank expression must have given me away, so he clarified: "Mobile...Moby...Dick...Richard."

Oy. "Okay," I said. "You're in the pub...Richard. We're the blokes from back home. You're halfway through your second pint. Brag to us."

He was suddenly more playful, his body language looser. His tone of voice became more jovial, and his story was peppered with slang. At several points, he laughed aloud with glee. And when, at the end, he slammed his bottle of water (his "pint") down on the desk and took a little bow, his colleagues stood and applauded. The morning's sure cure for insomnia had become the afternoon's life of the party. It was "Richard" who needed to address the big guns on Friday, and—according to those in attendance—when he did, Calvert's performance was the mutt's nuts.

Secret Sauce

Brianna, a talent recruiting specialist at a European fashion house, had a talk to give to the leadership team, and she came to a presentation workshop. "I'm definitely an introvert," she said when we asked what she wanted to work on. "I don't really like speaking publicly—but I have to do it more and more. I know I need to connect with folks, to get them engaged and make an impression." We asked her to stand up and give us three minutes of her presentation. It sounded something like this, in a steady, monotone voice:

Good morning. I'm here today to talk with you about a change in our recruiting processes and to discuss how this is going to affect each of you and your departments. In the past all hiring has been done centrally with HR playing the lead role in the search through various social media outlets, on our website, through headhunters, and selecting candidates for the interview process, and then conducting all of the interviews. Then we do an identification of two to three candidates for you as department heads to meet with and interview, from which you then choose your top picks and let us know. We've been researching best practices, and the research shows that there is greater retention when the hiring is done more directly by the people and departments who will be taking in the new candidates.

And on. And on. The information was all there, and it was exactly what the audience needed to know—but that's where the connection ended. Brianna—the living, breathing person—was nowhere to be seen.

Kat Koppett, a dear friend and talented coach, facilitator, and designer, was leading this session. Quick comment about Kat: She has her own training company (Koppett and Co.), and I am always trying to get her on a project in the midst of her busy schedule. We (and Brianna) got lucky this time. Kat decided to use a time-honored acting technique—the *as if*. She directed Brianna to perform exactly the same presentation, but this time to tell us a *story*, and to do it *as if* the story were top secret.

Embarrassed at first, Brianna took the leap as she leaned in and began to whisper. Immediately, the audience leaned forward as well (always a good thing). And Brianna's entire performance changed, including even the content.

Good morning (Brianna whispered). *I've got something small but important to share with you today. I hope I can speak frankly.* (She looked around to see who might be overhearing.) *It's about our recruiting process. Back in the day, your predecessors used to be more involved from the get-go. It turns out that the people they hired stayed longer. In fact, some of those people are... you.* (She smiled, paused, and spoke even more quietly.) *So we're looking to bring this back, making use of the technology that exists now, and we're piloting it with you guys, so don't tell anyone else about it yet...I mean, who knows if it's actually going to work again. It could be just a bit more work now, but so much less in the long term! I have a good feeling about this.* (She paused again.) *But what do you think? I'd need your help to give it a try.*

Suddenly there's suspense, tension, laughter, interest, and involvement between Brianna and the audience. Now, instead of being told a set of facts, we're being invited in, included. We're hearing a story, and as with any good story, we want to know what happens next. The fact that what happens next directly involves us makes this a *very* interesting story.

Kat wasn't suggesting that Brianna should pretend the policy is a secret when she tells the story in her actual presentation. But the very real performance that the "secret" produced—her conversational, somewhat playful style, her high degree of attention to the audience, the new ways of explaining the process she discovered? She can use it all.

Growing Through Stories

When we ask people to do a different performance than what they would normally do, like to give their talk as if *this is the best news ever,* or *you're talking to an audience of five-year-olds,* or *you're a fiery preacher doing the Sunday sermon,* they surprise themselves. They surprise one another. We've had people who were awkward and stiff transform in ways you could never ever have guessed. People who can't bear to be separated from their data points come alive. Suddenly, they gesture freely, their faces become expressive, they fill the space. They're not just some everyman or everywoman, sitting in a chair telling a story. They choose how to stand and speak, when to be quiet. They look at the options for expression and deliberately decide which of them to use in each moment. A new performance direction/character, either for a typical business presentation or for an already interesting story, automatically brings to life all kinds of possibilities that you don't even know are there.

In our work with clients on performing as storytellers, the coaching and the direction we've given have been as varied as the stories and the people themselves. But there are a few principles that make these performances effective, and I want to share them with you:

1. **Be brave; share something personal and meaningful to you.**

   The success of Charlotte's story depended almost entirely on her making this choice. More often than not, there is a way to connect something about you personally, as well as the business objective at hand. It takes some exploration and support, but it's well worth the effort—for you personally and professionally, and for us, the audience.

2. **Paint a picture; provide detail and color.**

   Think of your story as made up of two elements: the forward motion of the narrative (this happened, then this, then this, etc.) and the color (everything else, including descriptions, sounds, smells, and emotions). To keep Ugga engaged, Ogg let her see every twig in the forest, every twitch in the dik-dik's face.

3. **Include your audience.**

   Ask yourself, *What role do my listeners play in the story I have to tell? What's their stake in the outcome?* Brianna turned her audience into the hero of the story that was about to unfold, and in return we felt inspired to act the part.

4. **Mix it up; start in the middle of the action.**

   Compare these two opening passages:

   a) *On March 9, 2016, I participated in a workshop with Performance of a Lifetime. It took place at our Florham Park office.*

   b) *I had never been so scared in my life. There I was, standing on a stage in front of my entire department...*

   Which one makes you more likely to lean in? This "start in the middle" technique has been perfected by the pros in the TV business, who get paid to capture our eyeballs immediately lest we change the channel and miss the ten minutes of ads that follow the opening sequence. And it's not limited to a narrative story per se—turn back to the first page of this chapter, and notice how it starts. No preamble, no explanation; you're just immediately involved.

5. **Act it out; play different characters.**

   Ogg's story depended on this completely, in large part because he had the particular challenge of lacking the power of speech. Calvert started out depending exclusively on his verbal ability, which ended up sedating his audience. His dormant talent for bringing a crowd to its feet was unleashed by his shift to another character—

one he was very familiar with and that allowed him to be much more expressive.

6. **Answer the question: What do you want your audience to think, do, and feel?**
Each of our storytellers had very specific answers in mind—take a minute to reread their stories and see if you can identify them. Then, when you craft your story, start with your own answers. Then think about your audience again: What do they *currently* think, do, and feel? What's the difference between their answers and yours? The journey between them can provide much of the raw material for a story.

Becoming a great performer of stories has many benefits, not just in business but in life—from regaling co-workers around the watercooler to entertaining a potential spouse; from making a presentation that lands a big account to convincing a middle school to accept your kid; from letting your organization know just how good you really are to inspiring your employees to take on a new challenge or getting them to care about something they didn't know they needed to care about.

But there's another benefit, maybe less immediately visible, and to me it's a big part of why I care so much about your storytelling performance. Activating your ability to tell stories can also be a way of reigniting learning and development, both others' and your own. Yes, most stories have a beginning, a middle, and an end. But stories are also ongoing. They can change as we change, and we are changed by them. Even Alice in Wonderland knew that. We learn and grow as we reconsider them and when we tell them to others. Charlotte, Calvert, and Brianna all had stories before we met them. But by performing their stories, they also created brand-new stories. About who they were and what they were about.

So what's your story?

Back in the prologue to this book, I brought up the idea of creating your own personal board of performance directors. If you haven't done that yet, now's the time. Your board need not be big (one or two people would work), and they don't necessarily need any special skills. They should just be folks you trust and who are open to—at least at first—simply joining you in some of the exercises you're about to see. Though it's definitely not required, if they're interested in reading the book, too, that'd be great, because then you can be on *their* board.

We're All Storytellers Exercises

1. Experiment with your own story: Introduce yourself at a networking event, a cocktail party, or a dinner—in new ways. Instead of simply saying your name and the usual stuff (where you work, what you do or your title, who you know, what you've done, etc.), include in your performance the words *I believe*, or *I've always thought*, or *I feel*. Use different lines with different people so that each conversation will be varied.

2. To begin "storifying" a business presentation, write/conceptualize/ experiment with it by starting with the line "Once upon a time...," and taking it from there. Improviser/storyteller Kenn Adams's "Story Spine" expands on this idea, and to learn more, pick up the book *Training to Imagine* by Kat Koppett.

3. Tell a story to a friend and ask her to be your story director. Every time she wants to hear more details, she interrupts you and says, "Color," at which point you add color, such as "*The road was made of old cobblestones, which had been worn down by years of horses and then automobiles.*" When your friend is satisfied with the detail, she interrupts and says, "Advance," and you continue the narrative of the story, such as "*And we took that road all the way to the restaurant in L'Orange where my adopted sister was waiting.*" And so on, with more coloring and more advancing.

4. Create/write/perform a story as three different characters. For example: Queen Elizabeth, Yoda, and your favorite colorful relative. Insist that a few friends sit around and listen. Invite them to do the same.

Those Challenging Conversations

Let us make a special effort to stop communicating with each other, so that we can have some conversation.
                                                                    —*Mark Twain*

You're about to give one of your direct reports a performance review, and it's not good. To make matters worse, until your recent promotion, this person was your peer.

———

Your work on a project for a client has well exceeded the original scope. You're already far into the additional work, and you haven't talked to either your boss or the client about it.

———

You've heard that a colleague who is also your friend told your boss that a deliverable was late because you were insisting on changes near the very end. This isn't the first time he's tattled on you. Before this recent incident, you scheduled drinks with your friend... tonight.

———

Part of your job as a doctor is to have conversations about DNR (do not resuscitate) orders with patients. These always stress you out, and you've been dealing with them by getting through them as quickly as possible.

———

Your new, young assistant is talented and very enthusiastic. One of her responsibilities is to capture the action steps from your meetings within twenty-four hours. It's week four and you've had to ask her for these every week so far.

———

You work in an office where your boss is an old-school man's man. He calls all the other men in their office by their names. But he insists on calling you, the only woman in the office, "honey."

———

Out of the blue, your client announces that a yearlong project has been canceled in midstream. She's unwilling to talk about it, and a great working relationship hangs in the balance.

———

A colleague you like and respect wants to "share" a client, which means less commission for you. You don't want to appear selfish or uncollaborative, but you were the one who got the client in the first place.

———

I thought about naming this chapter "Valuable but Seemingly Unlikely Opportunities to Grow Personally and Professionally While Strengthening and Building Your Relationships." Wordy and not very catchy, I know. But here's why:

What we call things makes a difference. Ludwig Wittgenstein, the brilliant twentieth-century Austrian philosopher, said, "The limits of my language mean the limits of my world." The words we use to describe something don't simply name it but often contribute to our experience of it—how we understand it and how we feel about it. "Challenging" and "difficult" aren't neutral terms. Labeling conversations with those words sets them apart from and outside of what they actually are. They are conversations. With and between real human beings. With a lot in common with all the other conversations in all the varied scenes of our lives. Some conversations certainly evoke particular emotions, raise particular challenges, or require particular performances. But they all exist on the continuum of conversations that make up the scenes of our plays. I'm not saying this makes them easy. I'm suggesting that if we don't segregate them out into a special category, they can be less of a boogeyman. We're still all people, doing the best we can as we perform and improvise all the scenes of our lives.

Okay—so that's why I don't like the name of the chapter. What's with this "seemingly unlikely opportunities blah blah blah" stuff? Like

I said—language matters. It might be tempting to approach this chapter as a kind of survival guide for getting through challenging conversations, and we've certainly helped people with that, thousands of them. But many of our clients have discovered that approaching these conversations as opportunities for growth and relationship building actually changes what they are. So I urge you to use these stories, philosophical musings, and the exercises at the end to continue your growth as you make your way through your challenging conversations. As you experiment with new and different performances in them, you're going to learn a lot about yourself and others in the process.

"It means we need to talk."

Meet the New Boss

Cheryl had recently been promoted into a newly vacated and hotly contested regional sales manager position at an airplane engine manufacturer. One of her new reports, Melissa (who used to be her peer), had also applied for the position. Since Cheryl's promotion, Melissa had barely spoken with her. When it came time for Cheryl to give Melissa her third-quarter performance review, the picture wasn't pretty. Melissa hadn't made her numbers for three quarters running, and based on what Cheryl could see in the file, their former boss neither spoke with her about it nor let it affect her rating. When she tried to do both with Melissa, it did not go well.

That was on Friday. Cheryl attended the first session of a workshop on challenging conversations on Monday, and she volunteered immediately when we asked if anyone had a conversation they wanted help with. She talked us through the "scene":

> **Cheryl:** As you know, this is your performance review, and I'd like to talk about a few things. Let's start with your numbers.
> **Melissa:** Uh-huh.
> **Cheryl:** You've been under goal for the past few quarters. This is clearly a problem, and I'd like to discuss what you see as the issues.
> **Melissa:** Yeah, well. We lost one of our salespeople. I expected this to happen.
> **Cheryl:** And so what are you doing to deal with this?
> **Melissa:** Um, looking for a new sales guy? What do you think I'd be doing?
> **Cheryl:** Well, yes, I assume you'd be doing that, but that doesn't deal with the previous two quarters. Your numbers were off there as well, and so you need to address that.
> **Melissa** (*with sarcasm*): What a good idea.
> **Cheryl** (*with rising annoyance*): Look, Melissa, I'm trying to do your review, if that's okay with you.
> **Melissa:** Whatever. Do what you have to do.
> **Cheryl:** What is your problem?
> **Melissa:** I'm looking at it.
> **Cheryl:** This meeting is over.

Well. That certainly didn't go well. Still, I saw a "Valuable but Seemingly Unlikely Opportunity to Grow Personally and Professionally While Strengthening and Building a Relationship."

"Okay," I said. "Let's break this down a bit. What was your goal for this conversation?"

Cheryl thought for a second. "I guess the most important thing was to start to address her underperformance. I needed to tell Melissa where she stands and—unlike her previous boss—let her know the truth of her situation." She began ticking items off on her fingers: "Fact: her numbers are down. Fact: her underperformance is chronic. Fact: her rating is going down."

In their best-selling (and oh-so-helpful) book, *Difficult Conversations*, Sheila Heen, Douglas Stone, and Bruce Patton write, "Difficult conversations are almost never about getting the facts right…They are not about what is true." I couldn't agree more. And "what is true" is dangerous ground to stand on in any event. At the risk of wandering waaaaay off our subject, "truth" has been explored and debated and deconstructed by philosophers for centuries. Personally, I'm in the postmodernist camp that challenges the idea of absolute truth and the sanctity of truth altogether. Wars are waged in the name of truth—by all sides. People are hurt and hurt others in the name of truth. So I'm pretty wary about invoking truth to explain or defend or understand our differences, disagreements, or challenges. You have yours, I have mine, and neither of them have anything to do with building a productive conversation or taking care of our relationship.

And while "Just the facts, ma'am" might have worked as a catchphrase on the old TV show *Dragnet*, in real life it falls short. Citing, relying on, and righteously standing by "the facts" in the absence of working on what's needed to help you and the other person to move forward, together, is both problematic and *very* common. The conversation between Cheryl and Melissa is a good example of how naming the facts can get you nowhere. If Cheryl was going to be able to successfully work with (and provide leadership to) Melissa, she would have to get beyond the facts. So I asked Cheryl and the rest of the group what "offers" they had heard coming from Melissa.

"No offers whatsoever," Roger, one of the participants, said.

Others agreed. Just a truly unpleasant situation all around.

But then Maya, another workshop participant, spoke up. "I don't know about any offers, but I think Melissa is getting a raw deal here. I mean, she didn't have a great quarter, she lost her sales guy, she got passed over for promotion, and her former friend is now her boss and trying to act like there's nothing weird about them having this conversation."

Now we were cooking with gas. I pointed out to the group that everything Maya had just said was an offer in the scene—some had been made explicitly; others had been implied through attitude and emotion. All could be built with. We quickly identified a number of new performance opportunities for Cheryl to explore:

1. Bring up the elephant in the room: It's a boss/subordinate relationship now. That's a big change. Both of them are thinking it, but no one's saying it.
2. Cheryl has a new character to create, a leadership character that she'll have to grow into, and it's called for right now. How does she want to perform this new role?
3. And speaking of leaders, the former boss didn't seem to be much of one, having never spoken to Melissa about her results or reflecting it in her ratings. What's a different kind of leadership Cheryl can provide? How can Cheryl help?
4. Make the shift from seeing this as a "challenging conversation" to one that is an opportunity for growth, learning, and strengthening a relationship. Can Cheryl be curious and learn more about Melissa's situation so that she could potentially be of help? Can she become an ally to Melissa instead of contributing to her humiliation? Not be provoked by Melissa's attitude, but work to accept and build with it? Bigger still, can she begin to design a new way to approach leading the sales team?

Cheryl agreed to try it all, and when she returned for the workshop session the following Monday, she was in a much better mood. I asked what happened when she spoke to Melissa, and Cheryl walked us through the very different performance she (and ultimately Melissa) gave:

Cheryl: Melissa, I'd like to do a "take two" on our last conversation about your performance review. I want to start off by acknowledging the elephant in the room.

Melissa: And what's that?

Cheryl: Well, it's pretty obvious that this is awkward for both of us—not just my being your supervisor now, but also giving you a performance review.

Melissa: That's for sure.

Cheryl: Yeah, I should have brought it up when we spoke last. I'm sorry about that. Obviously I'm glad I got this promotion, but I hadn't really thought about how you'd feel, or how this kind of conversation might go. I know it's hard for me...but it's probably harder for you.

Melissa: Yes, it is. I'm not happy about it at all.

Cheryl: I understand that. But this is what has happened, and now we need to deal with it together. It's not a comfortable situation.

Melissa: No, it's not. But it's not anything you did. I'd have taken the job, too, if I'd gotten it.

Cheryl: Yes, I suppose so. And so here we are. Are you ready to dive into the performance review?

Melissa: Okay.

Cheryl: So we need to talk about your numbers for the year so far and what to do about your shortfall. Unfortunately, it's going to affect your rating, and there's no way around that. How's it going finding a replacement for Pete, your sales guy?

Melissa: Not great, actually. HR hasn't really turned up many good candidates.

Cheryl: Oh, that's not good. Let me reach out to them about this. Maybe I can light a fire under them. And I'd like to see if I can help you turn the numbers around overall. Do you have thoughts about how I could help?

Melissa: I do. And I appreciate it.

The conversation continued from there and apparently went pretty well, especially given its lousy "take one." Cheryl made a strong performance choice right at the top—she "went into the cave," as we say in our improvisation tenets, straight at what she previously had been avoiding altogether. She listened to the offers from Melissa, and rather than being reactive or defensive (especially to the "crappy" offers), she accepted those offers and built with them. Cheryl performed as a leader, not just a manager or a boss, by being direct on the one hand but also being curious and learning what was going on for Melissa, which enabled her to immediately see ways she could be of support (shades of follow the follower). They were paving the way for a collaborative (i.e., ensemble) approach to improving Melissa's sales numbers. Cheryl wasn't letting her off the hook but rather starting an engaged dialogue that would put the work on more solid ground.

Life and Death

Cheryl thought that facts alone should change a bad situation. Others use facts as a smoke screen, diverting attention from how uncomfortable they are as they speed through a challenging conversation hoping that whatever they manage to do will suffice. When I met him, Dr. Raj was like that.

There's probably no more challenging a conversation than discussing a DNR when you or a loved one has a terminal or life-threatening condition or illness. DNR stands for do not resuscitate—as in, if your heart stops beating or you stop breathing, the hospital or doctor is not allowed to "call a code" (i.e., to try CPR or artificial means of breathing to revive you). Over the years POAL has done a lot of communication training with doctors, including around this very stressful conversation, which most hospitals require any time a patient faces significant risk of death.

Recently, I was coaching a first-year resident named Raj. Several of his patients had given permission to be videotaped for training purposes, and one of them was a forty-one-year-old woman named Dara. She had two school-age children, was divorced, and, among other acute issues, had stage IV breast cancer that had spread to her bones and liver. Her deteriorating health necessitated an immediate DNR conversation.

I watched the video of the conversation. Raj entered her hospital room and launched in: "Hello, Ms. Brown. According to hospital rules, I am going to need to discuss your code status with you. Do you want to be a full code or a no code?"

Dara looked at him with concern and confusion. "I'm sorry, Doctor, I don't know what that is."

"It pertains to whether you want a DNR order."

"This is about dying? Oh, God. I have small children, I don't want to die."

"Okay, so you want to be a full code?"

Dara hesitated, then replied, "I guess so."

"Thank you, Ms. Brown. A nurse will be coming in soon to take some blood," Raj said, and he left the room.

On the video, I could see Dara begin to cry.

When we met later, Raj told me how uncomfortable he had been having the DNR conversation with Dara. That was why he fell back on the facts cloaked in medical jargon in order to get through it. But this tactic did nothing to alleviate his discomfort, and equally, if not more importantly, it was horrible for Dara.

I asked him what he feared the most about these conversations. He thought about it for a few seconds, and answered quietly, "Their emotions, when they get upset."

"What is it about their being upset that frightens you?" I asked.

"That I won't know what to do, or will make it worse, or..." He trailed off.

"Or...?" I prompted.

"Or it will make me upset."

"And what would happen if that happened?"

He was silent. "I'm not sure," he finally said. "But it would not be good."

"I want to show you something," I told him, and I turned on the video of his meeting with Dara. We watched silently as he and she spoke, he left the room, and through the twenty seconds or so before a nurse came in and turned off the camera. We watched Dara sitting alone crying until the screen went dark.

Raj turned away from the screen. "I'm so sorry," he said. "I didn't realize."

"Obviously you didn't," I said.

"I'm an insensitive idiot," he said.

"Well, you might have been then, but that's not what I'm seeing now, Raj," I said. "What I'm seeing—right now—is a doctor who cares about his patient."

"I do," he said.

"Okay. So as that guy—as the doc who cares—how would that scene start with Ms. Brown?"

After thinking for a bit, he said he would have asked her who she wanted or needed to be involved in this conversation. Did she want to make this decision alone? Did she have questions for him? Did she need more time to think about it? These, he said, were the kinds of questions he would have wanted a doctor to ask him or someone he loved.

Someone he loved. The idea resonated for Raj and led him to the realization that he could play a different doctor character than the one he had been playing. He could perform as a doctor who loves his patients. He has tried it several times since then, and he tells me that it has expanded what it means to him to be a doctor, that it has reminded him of why he wanted to be a physician in the first place. He's no less of a doctor, but much more of a healer. And while discussing a DNR with a patient is not a scene he looks forward to, it's one that he now is taking part in responsibly, with compassion and care.

Apology Necessary

And while we're talking about doctors and patients, here's another situation that brings challenging conversations in its wake: medical error. The conventional wisdom in the health-care industry is that when doctors make mistakes, they should never apologize—to patients, their families, anyone. The thinking is that by admitting the mistake, the apology opens the door to litigation. I learned otherwise from a colleague and amazing doctor, Sigall Bell, who does communication training with doctors at Beth Israel Deaconess Medical Center, a teaching hospital for Harvard Medical School. She and a growing number of others have been researching and practicing a radically different way of approaching mistakes, and the results are eye-opening.

The University of Michigan Health System launched a disclosure program in 2001 that encouraged doctors and health workers to acknowledge and apologize for medical errors. The results were impressive: The monthly rate of claims, or requests for compensation, decreased by 36 percent. Monthly malpractice suit rates dropped as well—by more than half. Finally, the average cost of the lawsuits filed fell from $405,921 to $228,308. By offering a sincere apology and compensation, the hospital staff were able to transform the emotionally charged standoff between wronged patients (and their families) and culpable doctors into a shared relationship of reconciliation, with both sides working to help the other. Another winning argument in the case for looking beyond the facts, the truth, and who was right and who was wrong. Instead, we can look to what's best for the relationship or the project, and then perform the conversation with this goal in mind. And, hey, maybe you won't be sued...

Heroes and Villains

Tony is an executive education consultant and a business colleague of mine. We've partnered together on many programs over the years, and

I've always liked working with him—he's a super instructional designer and facilitator. Several years ago he was working with the learning and development group at a global energy company, whose chief learning officer, Linda, had hired him to overhaul their onboarding program. Tony had brought POAL in to deliver a portion of the program, and so he kept me in the loop as he worked with Linda over several months to develop a curriculum, test classes with a sample cohort, fine-tune the design, and then prepare and train them as faculty to lead the rollout.

It had been a complex, creative, and arduous process, and Linda had been a great partner throughout—smart, highly opinionated, and hardworking. Not that their working relationship had been a walk in the park; they'd had plenty of bumps and collisions along the way. But they'd worked them through, and at long last a pilot group of trainers was primed to take ownership of what they had created.

But a challenging situation was about to unfold. Three weeks before the start of the pilot training delivery, Tony and the client team were meeting to make final preparations.

But Linda wasn't there. Her chief of staff had dropped in at the beginning to say that Linda was going to be late and to start without her.

Then, five minutes before the scheduled end of the meeting, Linda came into the room. She walked to her empty chair but didn't sit. Looking directly at no one, she said, "There's been a change in direction around training. Effective immediately we're suspending work on this program and shifting our efforts to implementing—" (Here she rattled off a long acronym that Tony didn't recognize; he assumed it was some kind of training process or model.) There was stunned silence in the room. Linda continued, "We'll meet again next week to get that under way." She turned to Tony. "Sorry. There's a new sheriff in town," she said, and turned to leave the room.

Tony was on his feet and following her immediately. He couldn't believe what he had heard—it must have been a misunderstanding. "Linda, this is idiotic," he said as he caught up with her near the restroom. "Stopping this now means everything we've done to this point—your investment, our work—will be wasted."

Linda abruptly stopped walking and turned to face him. "You think?" she said.

Tony plunged ahead. "The internal marketing for this is in full swing.

There's already a buzz about it. You stop now, and it both looks and *is* really bad. If your folks don't start delivering the new curriculum, they're not going to be able to get good at what they've learned. And it's a complete letdown for the pilot group. I don't think you understand the implications, Linda."

"You have no idea what you're talking about, Tony." She was yelling now. "I'm handling a lot of different priorities here." She opened the door to the women's bathroom. "May I?" she barked as she turned and walked in.

Whoa! Tony had been totally blindsided. First by the news of the project cancellation, then by Linda's response, and then finally by the e-mail he received late that night from her: "Hi, Tony. Sorry about yelling at you today. Well, sort of sorry. I don't like being called an idiot and I don't like being ambushed."

That stung. Tony read on.

"There is a lot going on around here that has led to this decision, and you know nothing about any of it. Aren't you supposed to be helping me?"

Tony called me the next day and told me the whole story. When he finished his blow-by-blow account, he sighed. "I really don't know what to do," he said. "I can't believe she's talking to me this way! Of course I'm trying to help her. To protect *her* investment, to keep *her* from looking bad, and to look out for *her* people. And somehow I've managed to get her pissed off. What am I missing here?"

"Shall I be blunt?" I asked.

"Shit," he mumbled. "Yes."

"Okay," I said. "In this drama, the story line is that you save the day, defend the people, protect the client's investment, protect your investment, and in the process show Linda that you care more than her. Is that about right?"

Tony was silent for a moment. He finally replied, "Yup. That's about right."

Some theatrical deconstruction: Tony and Linda had been in a play together—the same ensemble production—for more than five months. Then, the day before, there was a plot twist. And what did Tony do? He walked off the set and started a new play, with himself as the star. His role: the Hero. Which of course meant that Linda was now the Villain, so they were now Enemies. And right up until that moment, Tony had been *absolutely sure* that he was right and Linda was being an ass.

"Seems like you've got a choice to make. Your own play? Or get back in the one you and Linda created together?"

His answer was immediate: "Our play. Yup. I'm going to call her now." Tony was never one to hesitate.

He told me later that week that he had reached Linda right away. When he called she was clearly in the middle of a lot of stuff. He asked her if she had a few minutes. Grudgingly, she said yes.

"Linda, I blew it," Tony began. "Totally unprofessional of me to chase after you like that, and you're right, I don't know what's going on."

"No, you don't, Tony," she said, "and I don't know what you take me for. I know this sucks. You're supposed to help me figure out what the hell to do about it, not bust my chops because it's happening."

"You're right, Linda. I was caught off guard. I was upset and so I decided to play the hero and fight for the cause. I know we're on the same side. Really, I'm sorry."

There was silence on the phone. Tony held his breath.

"Well, at least you didn't follow me into the ladies' room." And then, finally, she chuckled.

"Nope," Tony croaked.

"Okay," Linda said. "Get me some options."

And that's what he did. They ended up doing a smaller pilot version of the onboarding program, which kept it alive and ready to go when the energy company was able. These challenging conversations? Very common for so many of us on both sides of the table. Tony had to get back on the side of his relationship with his client in order to move forward. He had to get back to performing in *their* play.

Challenge Accepted

All conversations—even the challenging ones—are improvisational scenes in which you are both a performer and a director. And as we've discussed, you can decide to not simply be in the scene but to perform as a co-creator of it. You can relate to these conversations/scenes as opportunities to grow. Even when you're angry, fearful, worried, or upset, if you choose to be generous and "Yes-and" the person you're in the conversational scene with, you gain access to a whole set of other characters. If you choose to be curious and a learner, you can do much more than just argue or disagree. Sometimes you need a take two. Sometimes you've got to work to get closer to understanding what's going on for you and what's driving your reactions. Sometimes you've got to put yourself in the other person's shoes, even if for a moment, to imagine a viewpoint other than yours.

And if you're not naturally the kind of person who makes these kinds of moves, you don't have to be stuck with your previously identified "real you." Instead, you can authentically work with the multiplicity that is you. Instead of these-are-the-facts Cheryl, Melissa got to meet the more generous, collaborative, and leader-like version of Cheryl. Raj could be more than a physician gathering information for the next medical protocol; he could be a physician who cares. Tony could (eventually) get over his initial reactions and upset and get back to being a problem-solving partner.

Does this mean that your conversations will now all end with an arm-in-arm stroll into the sunset with a string quartet playing in the background? Doubtful. But you do have an excellent shot at transforming your antagonist into your scene partner on the way to creating something new together in the challenging, varied, and unexpected play we call life.

Those Challenging Conversations Exercises

1. Perform curiosity. Seek out somebody at work with whom you regularly disagree. Instead of an argument or dispute, have a conversation with him in which you're being curious and a learner the whole time. Feel free to review the rules of the curiosity exercise in chapter 5 on listening.
2. It's all about listening and hearing offers. Relate to everything that anybody says or does as an offer, with which you have both an opportunity and an obligation to create and build. Even and especially all of the crap. Fundamentally, let what's best for the relationship or project lead you.
3. The next time you have a conversation coming up that you're dreading, enlist the help of one of the members of your board of performance directors. Read this chapter together, and then tell her what the conversation is about and rehearse it with her. First have her play you, and respond to her with everything you dread hearing. Then have her play the person you need to talk to, and you play yourself.

The Art of Selling, Networking, and Other Schmoozy Things

You miss 100 percent of the shots you don't take.

—*Wayne Gretzky*

It was two months into the school year, and Jo was holding her first parent-teacher conferences. The mother of Kimberly, one of Jo's best students, walked in: a tall woman in her mid-thirties, wearing a conservative but well-fitted suit and oversized expensive-looking sunglasses. Jo introduced herself and showed her a seat. The woman looked at it, then at her (at least Jo assumed she was looking at her—she hadn't removed her shades).

"Do you have an adult-sized chair?" she asked Jo.

Jo rolled her own chair out from behind her desk and gave it to her, then leaned on the edge of her desk. "Thank you for coming in, Mrs. Campbell," she began.

"It's *Ms.* Campbell, and of course I came in. I have some concerns," she said. "First off, Kimberly is bored. She finishes her homework in fifteen minutes. When I ask her what she's working on in class, she says things like '*They're* learning multiplication.' I looked in her book bag and I found this." She reached into her Prada tote and pulled out a copy of *James and the Giant Peach*. "Are you serious? This is a child who reads the *Sunday Times* with my husband and me every weekend."

Jo cleared her throat. "It's a very good book, you know—"

"Yes, it was extraordinary when Kimberly was *four*," she snapped. "You seem to have somehow missed the fact that she is a very gifted child."

"I haven't missed it. This is a class for gifted students—she wouldn't have been placed in it if she weren't."

"I see," Ms. Campbell said, removing her sunglasses. "So that's how you know, by her 'placement'?" She made the word sound like spoiled fish.

"Ms. Campbell, of course there's more to it than that . . . I've observed Kimberly over the semester, and she is very bright."

"You've 'observed' her," she said (more spoiled food). "I have to say I'm disappointed. When our older son, Luke, was in third grade two years ago, his teacher, Mr. Johnson, did a lot more than observe."

Jo took a breath. "Well, I've heard Mr. Johnson was a wonderful teacher," she said. "You know, he retired at the end of that year."

"Yes. I hope at least some of his methods have remained in place."

"Probably, but I'm actually not sure," she said. "Last year was my first year here."

Ms. Campbell arched an eyebrow. "So you're new to teaching?"

"No, I taught for the past six years at Maplewood Elementary."

"I see. *Maplewood.*" (There's that smell again.) "Frankly, I didn't want Kimberly to stay here once Mr. Johnson was gone. But my husband won that fight, and here she is. A decision worth revisiting."

Clearly frustrated, Jo replied, "Ms. Campbell, I'm a little at a loss. If you'd like to remove Kimberly from my class, and from this school, by all means go ahead. I wish you the best of luck."

"*And cut!!*" I shouted. "Give them a round of applause."

"Thank God!" shouted Sophia, the investment banker who was playing the role of Jo, the teacher. She slumped into a chair and shook her head. Melissa Delaney-del Valle, a terrific actor/coach who played Ms. Campbell and was my co-trainer in this sales workshop, smiled for the first time in five minutes and reached over to shake Sophia's hand.

"So that was pretty rough," I said, and many in the room chuckled. "Do any of you know this person?" There were nods, and somebody yelled out, "Wasn't she in *The Wizard of Oz*?" Another person added, "Her daughter goes to my son's school." And yet another one said, "That's my client!"

An Unusual Sales Conversation

This parent-teacher scene is one we use to bring the performance approach into people's sales and business development work. It was the brainchild of a wonderful colleague, Judy Rosenblum, the former chief learning officer at Coca-Cola and former president of the executive education firm Duke Corporate Education. Judy and I worked together to design an unusual and (we subsequently learned) very effective sales and leadership training for the managing directors at a global investment firm. The program brought together some of the best thinking on consultative selling with top-notch role-play and improvisation theory/practice. Judy dubbed the program "Hearing Offers, Developing Needs, Seeing Opportunities," and we've been doing versions of it ever since.

Why a parent-teacher conference and not a more recognizable sales interaction? Because it allows salespeople to perform outside their normal sales roles and their typical sales scripts. The challenge we give them is to make a connection and build a relationship under less than optimal circumstances. We can focus on behavior, their relationship-building skills, their ability to deal with objections, different personalities, and practice a kind of selling where they are learning people's needs and identifying opportunities. They also aren't selling anything, or so it seems.

Yet this is in fact a sales conversation. Ms. Campbell is the customer—an unhappy one. Jo's job is to sell herself as a good teacher for Kimberly, or her mom's going to shop elsewhere.

To Sell or Not to Sell

As Dan Pink says in *To Sell Is Human*, we're all in sales. No matter our official position—teacher, mother, technician, child, doctor, you name it—we're always looking to influence, persuade, or convince people to do things they might not automatically do on their own. And if you're worried that selling means being slimy or manipulative, never fear. The sales performance we're talking about here is much less about getting someone to do something and more about creating/discovering together what "the prospect" needs, what "the seller" has to offer, and whether and how those might be a match.

This idea may ring a bell if you're familiar with "consultative selling," the approach to sales in which you learn from your client or customer what their needs are, then offer products or services that meet or address those needs. It's considered a dialogue, as opposed to simply pushing your "ready to go" product or service. Of course you need to have done the work to elegantly and eloquently articulate what you have to offer, so that's always part of the picture. But side by side with the customer, you're learning about and simultaneously helping to shape/determine/decide what would be best for them.

"He doesn't just enjoy the water. He's always gotta work the pool."

On a recent visit to the cosmetics aisle, I experienced a range of approaches to selling. At one makeup counter, the salespeople started throwing product at me before I could even say why I was there, and I walked away with a large bag of mysterious samples that I will never open. At another kiosk, I was handed off to a different salesperson three times, each requiring that I explain what I was looking for all over again. (Apparently being a woman of a certain age was too confusing for one person to handle.) At the third counter, the saleswoman listened carefully, asked me questions about my current makeup habits and preferences, and then showed me a few different options. She was responsive when I didn't like some of them, and we figured out together what I needed. You can probably guess which salesperson I bought the most product from. Miranda was very good at consultative selling, and I now have the cleanser before the concealer, the primer before the concealer, concealer, the brush to apply the concealer, the powder after the concealer, the brush for the powder, and the concealer remover to show for it.

I never once had the feeling that Miranda was trying to get me to buy anything, mainly because whether she knew it or not, she was putting into practice some of the golden rules of improvisation. When you improvise onstage, you're never trying to get anyone to do anything. Instead, you're *discovering* what you're doing, and what there is to do, while you're doing it. In selling, you're using all that you know about your product and improvisationally co-creating an environment in which if there is interest and need, a sale can be made. Your priority is building a relationship and creating a conversation in which you hear offers—positive and negative—that you can act on. You're not actively listening so that you can make a sale, you're actively listening so that you can create with your scene partner. This might be hard for veteran salespeople to swallow, so I'll say it another way: You don't enter the conversation with the goal of making a sale. You enter with the goal of discovering whether you and this person might be interested in the same thing, with that same thing being something that you have to offer.

Even the best salespeople find that by focusing on the relationship, they discover far more opportunities to build with and act upon. I love watching the eyes of successful sales pros light up when they realize that they can now add this form of improvisational creativity and connection to what they've always done naturally. And it's a particular relief to many for whom networking doesn't come naturally to know that you can simply let yourself be impacted by the customer/client and that you don't have to force yourself on them.

Characterizing sales calls, networking opportunities, or other schmoozy things as performances gives us a way to understand what is actually going on: a conversation that is being co-created by human beings.

Jo and the Volcano

Back in our workshop, after explaining the underlying sales nature of the conversation between "Jo" and "Ms. Campbell," we introduced the idea of improvisational offers—emotions, body language, attitudes, and all of the verbal content—which can be positive as well as unpleasant, negative, even hostile. Considered from that perspective, Ms. Campbell was a veritable Vesuvius of offers: She's rich, she's picky about chairs, she's concerned about Kimberly's education, she's entitled and arrogant, her daughter is very bright, there's significant educational enrichment happening in the home, she doesn't trust or like Jo, she likes the book but thinks it's way below Kimberly's level, Kimberly is bored at school, she wants Kimberly seen as an individual rather than a cohort, she loved Mr. Johnson and his methods, and she and her husband weren't completely aligned about enrolling Kimberly. And likely more that I'm missing.

So much to respond to and build with! And for Jo to "make the sale"—to show Ms. Campbell she's a good teacher for Kimberly—she needs to both respond and build as a way to get closer to what Kimberly and her mother need.

We picked a few offers to explore: Ms. Campbell's concern and upset about Kimberly's education, the fact that the family is clearly engaged with her learning, and that they loved Mr. Johnson. I asked the group what "Jo" did to respond to these offers. The consensus was: not much. She was pretty consumed with dodging the bullets (as she called them) of arrogance and nastiness, eventually cutting her losses and walking away.

Ending the conversation when it becomes too unpleasant or unproductive is always a possible choice. But if you want to push further, to get past your own reactions to crummy offers (I talked about this in chapter 6, "Create with Crap"), you can do so by creatively building with them.

So what could our teacher have done? First, find a way to accept the mother's offers. Kimberly's bored in school? She reads the *New York Times*? Mr. Johnson was the One Teacher to Rule Them All? Rather than defend herself, Jo could have related to these as important information:

Ms. Campbell: *James and the Giant Peach*? Are you serious? This is a child who reads the *Sunday Times* with my husband and me every weekend.

Jo: That's very impressive! How long has she been doing that?

Ms. Campbell: Well, in a way, all her life. It's a tradition for us, Sunday breakfast with the *Times*, and once Kim could handle eggs Benedict, she was right there with us.

Jo (*laughing*): That's amazing. I don't know if we could get our twins to sit still that long.

Ms. Campbell: How old are they?

Jo: They turn three in January.

Ms. Campbell: Well then, give them a chance. Kim started with the magazine, just looking at pictures, but once she was reading she was unstoppable.

Jo: What's her favorite section?

Ms. Campbell: It's been "Arts and Leisure," but lately she's been spending more time on the "Week in Review" . . .

Jo: Ms. Campbell, I'm so glad we're talking about this. I like to get the class involved in some long-term group projects once they've gotten to know one another, and now I'm thinking a class newspaper is the way to go. How do you think Kimberly would like to be one of the editors in chief?

Jo's performance of curiosity allowed her to build with what she was hearing. She then was able to work to build a partnership with Ms. Campbell, to enhance and improve the learning experience for Kimberly.

Is this a sales performance? Yes it is. Creatively and improvisationally building a relationship with Ms. Campbell might lay the foundation for a trusting and valuable partnership, from which the "sale" could happen. Performing this character, and being both a performer and a director in this scene, makes that the focus.

Depth of a Salesman

I introduced Tom, a senior sales manager from an insurance company, back in chapter 5 on listening. He had put a relationship with a potential customer at risk and was looking for help on how to navigate the situation. The potential customer, Ella, was eager to move forward using their new product with a free trial. But Tom's company didn't give free trials. Worried that he might have led Ella to think they did, and not knowing how to win her as a customer, he just didn't call her back. That was clearly not a good strategy; the days were passing by, and Tom didn't know what to do about it.

When we asked Tom to rehearse a do-over with Ella, he went right to his memorized sales script ("Let me first say that you are an important customer to us and we really value your business"). Watching him deliver it onstage enabled his audience of peers to see that it rang false; he was doing an old-fashioned sales performance that was making things worse. We asked Tom and his colleagues to look at the offers Ella had given him. Someone yelled out that Ella was under a lot of pressure to get something *fast*. She needed Tom's help. Maybe, another colleague suggested, if he could address her need to get his product quickly, she would be open to not getting it for free. He needed to help her, not sell her. It turned out that Tom's colleagues were right on the money. When Tom called Ella, he asked about the time crunch and let her know that he could get her something quickly but not for free. Ella wasn't concerned about the price (she'd simply misunderstood about the free trial), and she was delighted that Tom could get something to her promptly. Ella's boss was on her tail, and she now saw Tom as a lifesaver, not as the salesman who didn't return calls.

Get Working on Networking

Michael, a senior VP in the office of the CFO for a national retail furniture chain, was at a new level in the organization where he needed to be networking at high-level internal events as well as at industry events. The industry events were easier for him; for the most part he was able to gather with fellow accountants who spoke the same language, but the internal networking events were a nightmare for him. He was intimidated by the C-suite guys. And though it was incumbent upon him to appear relaxed, to impress, and to seem to be one of the guys, Michael felt just the opposite—like a high school freshman in a room full of seniors.

Michael had been brought in to design and implement a new internal audit system for the entire organization. He needed buy-in and cooperation from the big players in order to make it happen, and he hadn't put himself in a position yet to make those connections and build relationships in a more informal way. Networking was going to be key. He needed to sell his program and himself to this seemingly impenetrable clique if he wanted to move the organization forward, build his own reputation and name, and get the credit he deserved. To help Michael network with the big guys, we designed a simulation of an internal event, an annual breakfast with everyone from the C-suite and other bigwigs. Eight actors played the people Michael needed to get up close and personal with: his boss, various business presidents, the head of HR, the general counsel, and other organizational luminaries.

Before beginning the simulation, we gave Michael a performance direction: He was not there to impress the leadership. He was there to *be* the leadership, with a central performance of generosity and graciousness, like a host. (To dig deeper into this performance choice, check out chapter 11 on performing with presence.)

Michael entered the room to find everyone sitting around chatting prior to the meeting. "Carson," his boss, saw him enter but didn't say hello and turned to speak with his back to him so that Michael was clearly excluded from the conversation. Michael's eager-beaver buttons had been pushed, and he looked like a puppy trying to get into the conversation. He kept inserting himself, reporting on great work he was doing even though nobody had asked. It was a bust.

We called an end to the scene. Jeff Flowers, one of our most seasoned coach/actors, gave Michael another direction: "You don't need anything to happen here today. So don't come after us. Say less, make a statement, and let it be our choice to come to you."

It took a few more tries before Michael really got it. This was a hard one. On take four, Michael came in, sat down, leaned in, and smiled and nodded, but he didn't say anything. He looked at his smartphone for a minute before putting it back in his pocket. He then said slowly and confidently, "How are you guys?"

"Carson" said in a very serious and self-important tone, "We're working on the financing of the VSI project."

"How's it going?" Michael asked.

"Slowly." The others around the table nodded very importantly.

"It's important," another said.

"Very," another chimed in.

Michael paused. "Hmm...," he said, then paused again. "My team is doing some work that's related to that. Would you want to see some of the shortcuts we've developed? It might help for you to get them early."

We all broke into applause. Eager-beaver Michael had been replaced by the smart, confident guy that he was (though never before among the C-suite). By being generous with his knowledge, instead of trying to impress and be included, Michael not only freed himself from his nerves, but he was able to actually listen to the conversations at hand and engage in them in a genuine way.

Shortly after our simulation, Michael found himself at a dinner sitting next to his (real) boss's boss—a scene that would have freaked him out if he hadn't been rehearsing for just this sort of scenario. With generosity as his MO, Michael was able to engage in a relaxed, comfortable conversation. It established just the kind of relationship he needed to gain the confidence and buy-in of one of his company's top leaders.

Dan Pink is right on point. One of the reactions we hear from people who take our sales and networking workshops is, "Wow, to sell really is human." They discover that sales and networking can be fun, nourishing, and can even allow them to feel or develop empathy for people for whom they previously had none. Of course salespeople still have to hit their numbers, and almost everyone in business is called upon to network if she or he wants to move up the corporate ladder or expand business opportunities. But if you co-create by listening and "Yes-and"-ing, you're going to build a stronger customer base, you'll enjoy your work more, and yes, you'll be far more likely to make a bigger sale in the end.

The Art of Selling, Networking, and Other Schmoozy Things Exercises

1. Prepare for a conversation/scenario in which you usually would be trying to make a sale (or influence someone, or get him to do something). Perform with the sole intention of discovering what's important to him. Don't try to make a sale.

2. Before your next networking event, ask yourself: *What kind of scene/play is this event going to be? What characters can I expect to meet?* Then create a character and a particular performance for yourself. Examples to consider:

   a) The Generous Host. You're there to make other people feel welcomed and comfortable.

   b) The Most Curious Person. You've come to learn who people are, what they do, and what's important to them.

   c) The Connector. Who are people you could introduce to one another? What connections can you offer to those you might meet in this context?

   d) Your Role Model. Someone you know whose style of networking or selling you admire or think is effective.

3. Work with one of the members of your board of performance directors to come up with three different ways to introduce yourself and your product or service. Pay close attention to how people respond. What feels good to you and why? Learn what seems interesting to other people and what doesn't.

4. Hear offers, develop needs, see opportunities. Rinse and repeat.

Perform with Presence

I gravitate towards gravitas.

—*Morgan Freeman*

In my building in Greenwich Village, there is a family I see in the elevator and in the nearby park all the time. They have two dogs: One is a massive goldendoodle named Sam; the other is a tiny four-pound Yorkie named Nelly. At the dog park, you'd expect everyone to gather around the giant goldendoodle. He's a beauty, with curly golden locks and a big smile. But they don't. All the dogs and all the people gather around the tiny little teacup. And no matter what Sam does to get attention, everyone just seems to ignore him as he lopes around looking slightly confused.

Nelly is tiny, but she doesn't act tiny. I've seen her pick up toys that are twice her size and prance around the park proudly with them bulging out from either side of her mouth as people laugh and point. Her prance seems to get even fancier the more people look and coo. I've also seen her take on dogs literally twenty times her size. Just the other day, she marched up to a hundred-pound Rottweiler, stood on her hind legs, and then chased him around the dog park as he looked back warily to see how close behind she was—you'd have thought a grizzly bear was after him. Pretty impressive. This little four-pounder obviously thinks she's an alpha wolf. She just has a certain special something that gets the attention of people and animals alike.

Nelly's got presence.

Like many of the topics we've been exploring in this book, presence has been discussed, defined, dissected, and dissertated about endlessly. Is it innate? Can it be learned? And for that matter, exactly what are we even talking about when we talk about presence? At the beginning of workshops we give on leadership presence, I often do a quick exercise to help bring this elusive quality into focus. I ask participants to think of someone who they think "has presence." The more the better. I then ask them to list adjectives that describe that person. Here are the ones that come up all the time: assertive, authentic, candid, charismatic, clear, composed, concise, confident, connected, courageous, credible, determined, energetic, funny, insightful, intelligent, open, passionate, poised, self-confident, sincere, thoughtful, transparent, and warm.

That's quite a list! Those words definitely describe someone you'd want to know and follow. And here's the thing: Every term on that list is an action or an attribute that can be performed and—the most important part—therefore developed. It's also the case that most if not all of us already have at least one of these characteristics. So rather than presence being another one of these innate abilities with which only a few are gifted, we can build with (Yes, and) what we already have available to us while adding new performances (again—Yes, and) to perform and develop our presence. And I'm not saying this just to make you feel better. Performing with presence is a creative, developmental dance; a weaving together of who we are and who we are not.

Amy Cuddy is a social scientist at Harvard Business School who as of this writing has the second most frequently watched TED talk. It's about her research on what she calls "power posing." Studying nonverbal expressions of power, Cuddy noticed that across the animal kingdom, and in the human world, too, dominant individuals pose expansively, taking up more space. But she wondered whether the reverse might be true as well: Could posing in a powerful way actually make you more powerful? Cuddy's research has shown that holding a high-power pose for two minutes (like standing with your arms in a V over your head or sitting back in a chair with your feet on the table) actually helps you become powerful, significantly raising the hormone that makes you feel more confident and lowering the one that makes you feel stress. In another experiment, she showed that job candidates who power-posed for two minutes before their interviews were rated as more appealing hires.

I'm not surprised by the results of Cuddy's study, and I really like that twenty-nine million–plus people have tuned in to TED to hear her speak so passionately about it. I think she's hit on something pretty deep and substantial, and her "power posing" exercise is the tip of the developmental iceberg. It's an important aspect of how we humans grow, learn, and change. We can perform a power pose—just as we can perform empathy or thoughtfulness. We can break away from our scripts, we can perform listening instead of arguing, and so on. When we perform with presence, we are engaging our developmental capacities, and that means we're making use of our bodies (which include our brains and hormones), emotions, intellect, social relationships, creativity, and more. Our performance choices inform how we feel, think, and interact; they affect how others respond to us; and thus they have a significant impact on who and how we are at work and everywhere else.

Presence for All of Us

Sir Laurence Olivier wrote in his autobiography that "the intimacy between the audience and me during the soliloquies in *Hamlet* and *Richard III*—we were like lovers." You'd be hard-pressed to find anyone with more presence than Laurence Olivier. But what's clear from this quote is that he understood the relational nature of his astonishing abilities. As do most performers worth their salt.

When we're brought in to help folks with their presence, one of the first questions we ask is: Who is your audience? Every room is different and requires a different performance of how you show up. Sometimes the scene you're in is a formal presentation where you're the center of attention. Sometimes the scene is a meeting with a client, colleagues, and your boss, and everyone is sharing the spotlight. Sometimes the scene is greeting someone you've never met before, and you're making a first impression.

Whatever the nature and style of the scene, perhaps counterintuitively, the best way to create, demonstrate, and perform presence is by *focusing on, and being generous to, others.*

Here's an exercise we like to use when working on presence. Early in a group workshop, when everyone is still feeling a little (or a lot) nervous and uncertain about what the day will bring, we set up a scene: It's the mingling hour before a business event. And we direct them to simply do what they would naturally do in that circumstance. They begin to mingle, all somewhat self-consciously. Some aggressively meet and greet as many people as possible, some talk to one or two people, some might stand to the side, and some connect halfheartedly if at all. At some point almost everyone glances over at the workshop leader to see if they're "doing it right."

After a few minutes, we stop them and give them a new direction (you'll recognize it from an exercise I just gave you in the previous chapter). It's the same setting, but now imagine that they're the unofficial host of the event, responsible for making everyone else feel comfortable and at ease. The new scene begins, and the room is immediately transformed. All the self-consciousness is gone. It looks like a mix of thoughtful, relaxed, high-powered, energized people enjoying themselves in this activity. Everyone has a presence that is unique and engaged. I end the scene with "Curtain!" and a boisterous conversation ensues:

"Wow. That was amazing. I have no idea why that worked better, but it did."

"I liked being responsible for other people. It gave me something else to do rather than obsess over how I was doing. I was too busy being attentive to others."

"I hope I can do this for real. I feel like I have about as much presence as a snail. What I added to my performance was asking questions and listening. I never do that. I don't know how it read to others, but I felt more there. More present."

The impact of defining and performing presence as relational is threefold.

First, look carefully at most of the attributes I cited earlier (warm, candid, open, passionate, poised, self-confident, sincere, thoughtful, composed, connected). Every one of those characteristics is defined by its relationship to other people. You literally can't do them alone.

Second, the relational performance of presence gets you out of your head. When you're facing and focusing inward, worrying how you look and sound, it's just about impossible to be energetic, warm, and candid, and you're not going to have much presence. But when you're facing outward—toward and with others—there's no room for the inward focus that saps your presence. So performing with presence is within reach and available to you. It's a choice, like all of the different performance choices we've discussed in this book, and there are many different ways for that performance to look.

And third, your outward attention provides you with the best possible way of making sure the "size" of your presence is appropriate to the situation. What do I mean? I demonstrate this with a simple exercise: In a roomful of people, I ask two people to face each other and begin a conversation, focused entirely on each other. They've already done the Generous Host exercise earlier, so they dive right in. After a moment, I ask them to step a few yards away from each other and continue the conversation. Instinctively, their voices become louder and their gestures get bigger. It's as if the narrow spotlight that had been focused solely on the two of them has now grown bigger. Finally, while continuing to converse, I ask them to become aware of us, their audience. And again we see a change in their presence. It's more subtle but detectable; it's as if their attention to us allows us to see them more clearly. This ability to scale our presence to fit our audience is not a technical trick. I believe it's intuitive, and all we need to unlock and make use of it is to focus on others.

You've Got What It Takes

Nicole has been in the media business for more than thirty-five years, and she has seen the industry change through its ups and downs. She started out as an editor, and over the years she has held a number of middle-management jobs, lived in many parts of the world, and worked for several different companies within the corporate organization. Nicole came to our workshop to improve how she came across when she was talking or presenting to audiences that were increasingly much younger than her.

Nicole began by performing a brief talk, a version of which she had recently given to a team of researchers and writers. During her presentation, she looked down a lot and spoke a little too quietly for us to easily hear. Those factors, among others, conveyed a vague sadness or defeat, a sense that Nicole felt we probably weren't interested in anything she said. I could see the impact she was having on her audience, and it wasn't good—they were somewhere between uncomfortable and uninterested.

As I watched Nicole, I worked to take in all that I had learned about her, even in this short amount of time. Right next door to this somewhat defeatist persona I also had the barest glimpses of a smart, accessible, very experienced professional, a Nicole who likely had a lot to teach and share.

I thanked Nicole for her presentation and then told her I wanted to bring out the experienced and wise woman that she is. She looked at me with a little smile and said, "She's been out of the office for a while."

"Well, her hiatus is over, Nicole," I said. "I want to hear and see *that*

Nicole give the presentation." I gave her some specific physical direction: Make eye contact with everyone at least once during her presentation, stand up tall, and when she moved, move very deliberately; pause on occasion and never look down. And right before she began, I added, "Be wise, be warm, and be 'with it.'"

She started the presentation again, and you could begin to see the barest glimpse of this "with-it" woman. Her presence was beginning to shift. I added some more direction: "Now I want some wisdom. Off-the-cuff, what are the two biggest lessons that you've had to learn as an editor? What would you like these younger folks to understand about this business that they might not know?"

I won't go into the details of what she said, but Nicole began to spin a tale that drew the room in. The story and the lessons were good, but her presence totally transformed. She had a dry sense of humor. She had an unusual blend of tough and warm. At the end of her presentation the room broke into applause, and then she was peppered with question after question. She handled those with an engaged ease and gravitas.

Sometimes, the way to create presence is to amplify parts of you that, for whatever reason (and there are lots of understandable reasons), you're having trouble bringing out. Performing yourself, even when you may not be feeling it, is the way to do it. When Nicole performed herself, she was able to be generous and give her wisdom, experience, and warmth. Nicole's "presence" just needed a little directorial nudge to see the light of day.

Try a Little Weirdness

Ed was a corporate finance guy at a management consulting firm. He was intelligent, thoughtful, and on the quiet side. When we met, he was having difficulty dealing with William, a senior partner in his firm, who was very opinionated and provocative. William liked to rattle cages. William's aggressive style and strongly voiced opinions really grated on Ed. He normally felt comfortable in his own skin, but around William he felt distracted and defensive, and he lost his sense of power in the face of such a brash, macho presence. Ed was not happy with how he reacted to William or how he showed up in the room for their conversations and meetings. Never particularly concerned with his presence per se, he now wanted to work on it.

After hearing this story, I asked Ed if he would be willing to try something that might seem weird. Ed responded with a twinkle in his eye, "The weirder, the better. I'm a gay, geeky quant-head, and proud of it. Bring on the weird."

Okay, he asked for it. "Remember John Wayne?" I asked.

"Sure," he said, and then in an exaggerated drawl, "Yooouu mean this guuuuuy, liddle laaaady?" We both burst out laughing.

"That's it!" I said. "Exactly. I want you to imitate John Wayne—not just the voice, but his swagger, too. Swagger like John Wayne."

When he stopped laughing he started striding around while swinging his shoulders and his hips. "You mean like this?" he drawled. He and I swaggered around the rehearsal room for a few minutes, periodically adjusting our imaginary Stetsons, dodging tumbleweeds, and gittin' those little dogies along.

Then I started playing his nemesis, William, and we improvised a scene. Ed played himself but maintained his swagger performance, and we had a five-minute conversation about decision analytics (I made up with obnoxiousness what I lacked in comprehension).

When it was over, Ed told me that he was feeling strangely freed up and relaxed, even though this performance was *so* not his style.

"Want to try it with William?" I asked.

"Sure," he replied, and pulled two imaginary revolvers from his imaginary holsters.

"Maybe not that big," I said. "But swagger nonetheless." Ed was game.

A couple of days later, Ed had the chance to test out his new stance—to meet swagger with swagger. He told me that instead of feeling defensive or bothered by his colleague, they'd had a particularly productive meeting. He didn't literally swagger, but the memory of swaggering gave him enough of a push to both feel and project the kind of presence he wanted. For Ed, the balance of power shifted back in his direction. Rehearsing a character that was very different from his own stretched him and provided a way out of the version of himself that he had gotten trapped in with William.

Ed and I did this work about ten years ago. As he charmingly tells it, he "swished and swaggered" his way to another firm where he's now a partner and goes by the name Eddie. And every time we see each other, his subtle tip of the hat and swing of the shoulders says it all. You're welcome, pardner.

*"It's company policy that we read your employee review in the voice
of Morgan Freeman."*

Present and Accounted For

Natasha, the executive from the financial services firm I introduced back
in chapter 2, wasn't conscious of her lack of presence. She would have
been content to remain in her own world as she entered her office every
day with earbuds in, shut off to everyone around her. Natasha was "on"
when she was performing in an official capacity, but when showtime
was done, her preference was to retreat back into her own world. That
might have been fine, but she was also ambitious and looking to advance
her career. Recently promoted to a much bigger job, her boss had high
hopes for her, and Natasha hadn't yet figured out how to fill these big
new shoes. She was understandably afraid that he was going to want her
to create a performance that screamed, "I'm here!," which felt like a leap
that she was not interested in or able to make.

We wanted to assure Natasha that big shoes didn't mean a performance where she had to be the center of attention now and always. But
she did need a performance that reflected her position and her growth,
and that would command respect for the many skills she had.

Maureen, her coach/director, suggested that her earbuds come out as
soon as she set foot on the commuter ferry landing. That she say hello to

the people around her who worked in her company. That she make eye contact in the elevator. This was the performance of an executive who took notice of and was interested in the people she worked with. Natasha didn't need to perform big. She just needed to take off her invisible shield and be the engaged, inviting person she was in more formal business settings.

Put another way, what needed to become larger in Natasha's case was not her character but rather the stage on which that already successful character appeared. Her promotion had provided her with that stage. Natasha then grew her presence by—literally—being present.

Name That Presence

Gravitas. Thoughtfulness. Connection. Attentiveness. Composure. Warmth. Assertiveness. These are all performance choices. Some may feel close to you. Some likely feel far away. What performance of presence do you want, and for which audience? How do you want to show up? As someone who can stay in the game with the most senior players? Who's thoughtful and serious? Who can hold your own at dinner with your in-laws? Lead a meeting with investors? As someone who can be relied on to manage a large staff? Who can hold the attention of a roomful of skeptics? Both children and adults? All of these are performances of presence for the different scenes of our work and personal lives, with lots of different ways to approach them. Let's take some of the lessons from Nicole, Ed, and Natasha and put them to work for you.

Perform with Presence Exercises

Make use of your body and physicality—they are key factors for performing with presence:

1. Practice walking slowly and deliberately. Then stand still and relax. Do this as you walk around your office or workplace and when you are making a presentation.
2. Notice your posture—are you scrunched in any way, do you look down, hold on to yourself? Stand up straight and look around at people and the environment.

3. In your next presentation—whether to a group of five or five hundred—work to make eye contact with everyone. When you are speaking, look at specific people and allow yourself to finish a sentence while looking at one person.

4. Add silence to eliminate "um," "y'know," and the like. Rather than trying to stop saying "um" and "y'know," *add* silence and pauses instead.

Create your character with presence: Consider yourself the unofficial "host" of various meetings, gatherings, or conference/video calls. Your job is to make other people feel comfortable and at ease, even if they are perfectly fine.

Experiment with different presence performances: Think of a story to tell or a short presentation to give. It doesn't have to be particularly interesting or dramatic; in fact, for this exercise it's better if it isn't. Tell it once the way you ordinarily would. (You'll need an audience for this—your personal board of performance directors, for example—or at a minimum a video of yourself doing it.) Now tell it again, with the addition of an *as if* direction. Then try another one. How did it feel to perform this material with the directions? What was the impact on the audience? Here are some sample directions, but feel free to make up your own (or ask your audience for suggestions):

- You're very excited about what you're talking about.
- You're addressing a kindergarten class.
- You're hung over.
- This information is top secret.
- You're madly in love with someone in the front row.

Coach as Theater Director

The director must be an organizer, a teacher, a politician, a psychic detective, a lay analyst, a technician, a creative being...above all, he must understand people.
—*Harold Clurman*, On Directing

In 2002, actor Adam Grupper found himself doing something he never thought he'd be doing: He was on a Broadway stage in a rehearsal of Puccini's tragic opera *La Bohème*, singing—in Italian.

Adam is a veteran Broadway character actor (*Guys and Dolls, Into the Woods, The Addams Family, Wicked, Fiddler on the Roof*) as well as a familiar face on film and TV (and was soon to emerge as one of Performance of a Lifetime's leading trainer-coaches). But opera was a whole other thing. In fact, he *hated* it. I asked him why. "Not only had I never done an opera before," he recalled, "I had never *seen* one. I thought it was bombastic, false, filled with overwrought performances." He had avoided opera all his life.

Until one day his agent called with an audition opportunity for an unusual hybrid extravaganza: an opera designed for Broadway. Against his better judgment, he decided to audition, and, much to his surprise, he got the part.

Needless to say, Adam was not trained as an opera singer. Yet there he was, playing the part of Benoît, the landlord who descends upon the young bohemians on Christmas Eve to demand the rent. And as the rehearsal process intensified, this old hand at acting and singing on Broadway started feeling like an impostor—especially concerning the language. "I had to sing in Italian, and I didn't know Italian," he said. "It has lots of rolled r's and sharp consonants and subtle vowel sounds. What would the audience think? Especially the Italian speakers and the legions of opera aficionados who knew the score and libretto by heart?

This was the most revered opera in the world! Would they boo? Throw tomatoes?"

One day, before a preview performance, the director took him aside after a run-through of one of his big scenes, and he gave Adam a surprising direction. "The director said to me, 'I'm relying on your experience to drive that scene. The other performers are young and new and tend to lose focus and energy. But you've been around the block. I need you to always maintain your highest level of performance so they can all rally around that and bring up their performance as a result.'"

Rather than pointing out anything that wasn't working, which could have undermined Adam's confidence, the director instead highlighted his experience and presence as an actor. "He made me feel that I had a special, unique role to play as a leader; that my particular skills and experience as a seasoned Broadway performer were exactly what was needed; and that, in some small part, I was performing as his surrogate director in the field, leading my fellow performers by example. It was incredibly flattering. And it did the trick. I would have followed him anywhere."

So who was this uniquely empathetic, collaborative, and sensitive director? None other than Baz Luhrmann, fresh off the success of the film *Moulin Rouge*, a critical and popular hit that earned two Oscars and eight nominations. By this point Luhrmann had established himself as an extraordinarily talented director and creative visionary, and actors would have lined up to work with him regardless of how he treated them. Yet despite his stature, one of Luhrmann's most notable qualities, Adam recalls, was how kind and collaborative he was.

"He welcomed input from everyone in this enormous cast. It was more than sixty people, and even the children were encouraged to chime in. And he insisted that everyone—especially those with the smallest roles—come up with a backstory about their characters' lives outside of the opera. He wanted the stage to be full of life, with lots of strong, vibrant characters. And by doing it in this way, he gave us accountability and a huge investment in the show. He was extraordinarily generous."

Luhrmann was able to direct Adam so successfully because he related to him in totality—as both who he was (a seasoned, experienced actor) and who he wasn't (a singer of Italian opera) at the same time. Luhrmann's directorial leadership opened up an opportunity for Adam and for the entire cast, which included several other nonoperatic types, as well as people with limited experience on *any* kind of stage. "He made us feel like, *Of course you can do this, of course you can perform opera. I want you to bring* your *qualities to my operatic production.*"

The show garnered two Tonys and seven nominations. And Adam came away from the experience changed. "I fell in love with opera," he said. "Baz opened a whole new world to me. Not only did I get to do something I'd never done before, but what a gift it was, to be so closed off about something and then discover it to be rich and meaningful." In a 2001 interview in the *Guardian*, Luhrmann said: "I wouldn't take a directing job if I didn't think it was enriching life." I've always thought Baz Luhrmann did that for his audiences. Adam Grupper found out he does it for his actors, too.

Directing a Performance

Leaders and managers today are being asked not only to be the experts in their particular fields but to coach and develop the performances of others. For most, it's part of the job description itself, and it's a big challenge.

By now, I've established that everything that goes on in the workplace can be seen as—and arguably is—a theatrical performance. So when we teach people to become great coaches, we look to the art and craft of the great theater directors. The best directors attend to even the smallest details of a performance, like the shape of a gesture or the timing of an entrance or exit. But they also help their actors relate to the larger vision of the play, understand the scenes they're in, provide historical context, and give insight into what drives their character and how the other characters see/feel/think about them. Directors observe and take in what their actors give them and then creatively play with and build on it all. They amplify the performers' strengths. They take into account the performers' limitations. They look for where to stretch them. At the end of the day, the job of the director is to do everything possible to make sure the performers' work is the best it can be and that their work both supports *and is supported by* the overall production around them.

So as *your* director, in this chapter I'm urging you to look at and perform your role in your workplace plays as that of a coach/director. And not just any director—there are plenty of brilliant directors who produce amazing plays and movies and are dreadful to work with. Read any actor's

"Find your voice: Why do you, Randy Tubbins, want to return the sweater?"

memoir, and you'll find endless horrifying and entertaining examples. No, the directors I want you to emulate are those who work with their actors the way Baz Luhrmann does, embodying the Becoming Principle. The performers I know—to a person—attribute much of their best work to the good fortune of having worked with just these kinds of directors.

The Performance of Directing

A quick note about terminology. I'm deliberately avoiding any fine distinctions in this chapter between "coaching," "mentoring," and "giving feedback." They're all terms used to name the activity of helping others get better at their jobs. And while their definitions are certainly helpful, more often than not you're doing a mix of these in the course of each conversation, let alone over the course of a relationship. And the skills, mind-set, and practices I'll be presenting to you can and will come into play in all of them.

Now let me introduce you to some performers and their directors I've met in my work.

Carmen, the head of marketing operations at a fragrance and flavoring company, found herself having to coach Nolan, whom she hadn't hired. Baby boomer Carmen described Nolan as a "party-on-dude, don't take life too seriously" millennial, and they had never hit it off. Nolan had been promoted (way too early, in Carmen's view) as a result of his success as a creative marketer for a segment of their business. Intuitive, imaginative, and dramatic, Nolan (who had tried unsuccessfully to get Carmen to use his preferred nickname, Snap) couldn't have been more different from structured, organized, and methodical Carmen. In their interactions Carmen was judgmental and critical, hurling unanswerable questions like "Why don't you just do it the way I told you to?" and eventually devolving into barking ultimatums, which did nothing to help Nolan improve. And Carmen was miserable; her boss was clear in telling her she had no choice but to keep Nolan on her team. Carmen was at her wits' end.

———

Alan, the founder of a highly respected independent publishing house, was known throughout the industry as a wonderful mentor, and many of his staff had gone on to become leading editors and other industry professionals. He had hired his new assistant, Melanie, with high hopes. She was outgoing and quick to learn the ropes of a demanding job that required everything from managing the phones to reading and commenting on numerous manuscripts. Alan was pleased with her performance, but after a few weeks he seemed to be the only one. To everyone else on staff, outgoing came off as saccharine. And quick-to-learn included quick to learn how to manipulate the boss.

Nearly every day, Melanie was coming to work at least a half hour late, always arriving with a sob story that Alan didn't question. Other problems were starting to emerge as well, like memos going out unproofed (again, accompanied by elaborate excuses). While some of Melanie's work was quite good (her comments on manuscripts; her rapport with their authors), it eventually became clear even to Alan that something had to be done, and *he* had to do it. But Alan, a very nice guy, did not like conflict. Four months passed, the problems continued, and he still hadn't had a conversation with Melanie. He didn't know what to say to her—whether and how to coach her.

———

Liam was an "overall reporting partner" at an accounting firm. In addition to managing a large portfolio of clients and running a geographic region for the firm, he had several other partners as direct reports and was responsible for their ongoing professional development. One of them was Brian, a charismatic rainmaker with great client relationships who made the firm millions year after year. But Brian also made life miserable for everyone who worked for and around him. Good people had left the firm because of him. Brian was entitled, bordering on abusive, and a lone ranger, and his addition to Liam's roster meant Liam had his coaching work cut out for him. It was clear that Brian's financial results had led to his being treated with kid gloves and probably meant that he was there to stay as long as the firm could keep him. But his current performance was going to result in losing more of the firm's talent and, frankly, was a lawsuit waiting to happen.

Coach as Director Tenets

The directors I admire employ a creative, fluid approach that's responsive to what's needed in the moment, but that also supports the entire play. Just as important, after giving a direction, they observe what the actors do, learn from their performances, and continue to direct from there. Directors often bring a strong vision to the process. But that vision is synthesized with their ability to create a rehearsal and performance environment in which people know that they are co-creating that vision, that what they have to give will be respected and will be used. That's the kind of setting where people do their best work, and, indeed, the actor-director relationship has the potential to be a continually collaborative, emergent process.

To help in creating the same kind of process in the workplace, here are my top ten tenets of successful directorial coaching:

1. **Look at the Scene:** Pay attention to your coachee's/performer's character—both in the scene/situation they want help with *and* in how they talk to you about it.
2. **Direct the Scene:** Ask yourself, *What could this scene be?* With your coachee/performer, consider the different options; be creative.
3. **Keep It Real:** See the real person before you, not who you wish they were (and definitely not your "mini-me").

4. **Be Curious:** Ask genuine (not leading!) questions that help you get to know them, how they think and feel.

5. **Collaborate:** Resist the urge to always provide an answer. Practice being creative and relish the process of discovery together.

6. **Yes, And:** Accept your coachee's/performer's offers and build on them.

7. **"Yes-and" Yourself:** Notice your reactions to your coachee; work to use them constructively and creatively.

8. **Build Character:** Create your coach/director character and pay attention to your style and performance.

9. **Get Help:** Helping someone else to grow can be challenging, and you'll need intellectual and emotional support to do it (call that personal board of performance directors of yours). And being a good coachee/seeker of direction yourself means that you know what it takes to grow.

10. **Bond:** Make it a priority to build your relationship with your coachee/performer, and create an environment for learning, development, exploration, and discovery.

To state the obvious, these tenets are a useful guide, but clearly not a silver bullet. Coaching as a director is first and foremost a creative act. What this means is that every coaching situation and every coaching relationship brings its own offers and nuances and opportunities and challenges. Let me show you how the coaching played out with Carmen, Alan, and Liam so you can see just how the direction emerged—in ways I would never have predicted—out of the scenes and roles that our clients were playing.

Carmen: Developing a Coaching Character

Carmen's frustration with Nolan was impossible to ignore, and in my own coaching session with her, that's the scene we started with. We talked about how things had been going in the past few weeks with Nolan. Carmen let loose. "First of all, he's always unprepared. He barges into meetings late, often with some dramatic story about why he hasn't reviewed the documents that were sent in advance. Second, we sit through meeting after meeting and make decisions and plans—you know, the *work*—

and then the next time we meet he doesn't remember what we agreed on. It's ridiculous." She paused. "You want more?"

"No, I think we're good for now," I told Carmen, wondering how I was going to direct *this* performance (#7 "*Yes-and*" *Yourself*). I asked myself: *What is this scene, and what could it be (#1 and #2 Look at and Direct the Scene)?* Well, I want to help Carmen get into the director's chair, which she is clearly not in—she's in a "venting" scene.

"I know you don't want to be dealing with this situation at all, and believe me, I'm sympathetic," I said (#6 *Yes, And*). "It's a hard one, and I'm not sure what I'd do if I were you. Nolan very well may be the wrong person for the job. But since you can't do anything about that right now, let's keep exploring [#5 *Collaborate*]. I assume you know that what you have been doing has not been effective in helping or changing Nolan?"

Carmen gave me a *thank you for being obvious* look. "Uh, yeah. But what the hell can I do? I can't see any way to fix him or fix this. But bring it on, Director. You're looking at a desperate woman."

I wanted to help Carmen make a choice that was not about trying to turn Nolan into a version of herself (#3 *Keep It Real*), which sounded like what she'd been doing and effectively ignoring the real person who was now working for her (and who, for the record, was very good at a lot of things—just not what Carmen needed him to be good at). I also wanted to work on Carmen's own performance style, her "coaching character" (#8 *Build Character*).

"Does this come up in other areas of your life? People falling short of your expectations?" I asked (#4 *Be Curious*).

She laughed. "I have nine- and twelve-year-old boys," she said. "What do you think?"

"So what do you do with them when that happens? Yell at them? Berate them?"

The answer was a very definitive *no*. Carmen said that she always tried to be encouraging, even when they messed up, show them how they could do better, and then cheer them on when they did. So I asked Carmen to tap into her skill at performing as a parent. Not to baby Nolan, but to perform as a coach and act accordingly.

Carmen was skeptical. "Well, yes—I can do that performance with my kids. But I am *not* Nolan's mother," she said. "God help that poor woman."

"I know," I said. "But what have you got to lose?" Carmen agreed to do one meeting this way and then we'd talk.

Carmen's report back illustrates how a shift in performance can completely change a dynamic. While she found it initially unpleasant (and frankly pretty bizarre) to take on the role of "supportive mom" when faced with Nolan's incompetence, Carmen is nothing if not diligent, so she gave it her all. And what she found surprised her. She was able to see all sorts of things she hadn't seen before. The big thing was that she was able to see *Nolan*—not simply the person who was driving her crazy. She saw and experienced Nolan caring passionately about the work, and she realized that he wasn't a total doofus. Carmen's character choice (the one she had honed over the years at home) was antithetical to the kind of fury and frustration that had dominated her relationship with Nolan until then. With Carmen's encouragement *and* guidance (prior to this character change, Carmen had been unable to give Nolan any specific and constructive feedback), Nolan began to make progress. Would Carmen keep him on staff if she was given the choice? Probably not. But she no longer felt like she was walking around with an albatross calling itself Snap around her neck. She had added "coach" to her performances at work.

Alan: Growing to Help Others Grow

Sometimes the most helpful form of coaching is to tell somebody what they need to do, period. Many theater directors believe—with some validity—that during the week before a show opens the only directions you should ever give are "louder" and "faster." Back to our terminology discussion earlier—perhaps the most resonant term here is "feedback." But it wasn't in Alan's vocabulary yet. He had to learn how to give straightforward direction about what was okay and what wasn't. This made him very uncomfortable because to him it felt like he would be giving criticism, which makes people feel bad, which in turn makes him a bad person. As a profoundly nice guy who prides himself on helping people, he found this really hard. To grow as a coach, Alan would have to perform as someone who's comfortable giving this kind of direct, no-nonsense feedback.

To help him become more comfortable being uncomfortable, my directorial assessment was that he needed prepared lines in order to have a shot at getting through this conversation with Melanie at all, let alone doing it successfully. So I gave him some "straight talk" lines to use as a starting point, to guide and focus the improvisation. After figuring out where and when Alan wanted to have the conversation (in the conference room, at the end of the workday on a Monday), I gave him the first part of his performance: sharing an observation.

> *Melanie, I want to talk with you about some performance issues in your work. A lot of what you're doing is going well, and I'm happy and feel good about that. Today we need to talk about what's not going so well. You were late to work numerous times during the past month, and in the past few weeks you've let several memos go out without being proofread and corrected.*

Next he would describe the impact of what he had observed:

> *When you arrive late, it disrupts the team because others have to step in to cover for you and that takes them away from their jobs. It also has an impact on the overall environment of professionalism and respect for everyone's time. The memos going out with mistakes reflect very badly on the company, and on me personally, since two of them were from me.*

Then came some specific direction:

> *First, I need you to much more carefully proofread all of your work. For the next month I've asked Aisha to do a double check as well, because I can't risk any more mistakes on this. Second, I need you to be here on time, every day. I understand that on occasion things happen—and in that case you need to call me directly and let me know. But this cannot happen on any sort of regular basis.*

Alan memorized his lines and had the conversation. He reported that his worst fears came true. Melanie burst into tears. But knowing that this was a possibility, we had done some emotional preparation—working through Melanie's potential reactions and rehearsing a variety of choices in response—so he was ready to be kind (a performance he was quite adept at) but steadfast. The reality was that as hard as this was for Melanie to hear, from a developmental point of view it was exactly what she needed. And as hard as it was for Alan to do, it was an important moment in *his* development as well. Committed as he was to guiding and mentoring young talent, his liberal nice-guy posture wasn't helping this young talent one bit. And his memos finally started going out typo-free.

Liam: Co-Creating Development

Liam arranged to meet with Brian in Brian's office. He felt that since a candid conversation about Brian's performance would likely be difficult, the setting should be as comfortable for Brian as he could make it. Liam opened by sharing his view of the situation, almost verbatim with how I reported it to you. And then he said to Brian, "I don't know how to address this. I don't have the answer for how to help you change this scene and the character you're currently playing." (Liam had been an actor in musicals in his youth, and he loved the performance language we had reminded him of.) "I just know that we need to do something about this. As a company we've enabled you to be this way, so I think it's our job to figure it out together."

As Liam told me later, Brian's reaction was uncharacteristic. He was circumspect, and he didn't fly off the handle the way he typically would when challenged. "Brian really is a great problem solver, and I wanted to tap into that," he said. "Because I really *didn't* have the answer, I knew it had to be a shared project." I loved this because, as I said, the primary job of the director is to create an environment in which you, together with the actors, can discover what is possible and what is needed.

Liam's work with Brian took place over six months—six difficult months—so I can't share every twist and turn in the conversations and relationship. But let's fast-forward a bit. Brian had agreed to meet regularly with Liam and work to deconstruct and reconstruct specific scenes in which he was inappropriate and abusive. But his initial responsiveness faded when Liam started giving him specific performance directions. Liam had told Brian that he needed to apologize to an admin whom he had practically thrown under the bus because she had left someone off a calendar invite. "You're holding me down, man," Brian had snapped. "You're trying to hold me down." I asked Liam what he did in response.

"I just nodded and told him, 'I guess I am,' and 'Let me know how it goes.'"

After months of this kind of back-and-forth, Liam and I had one of our coaching-about-coaching conversations. He said that Brian would grudgingly do specific performances that he gave him, but Brian didn't seem to grasp that he had to make a total performance shift, that he needed to create a whole new character so that Liam didn't have to hold his hand (or "hold him down") every step of the way. I asked Liam if he had thoughts about what a new character for Brian might be. What was a character that would be a stretch but still be something Brian could do?

Liam thought a bit and then said, "By George, I think you've got it!" (It turns out we're both big *My Fair Lady* fans.)

I replied, "No, by George—I think *you've* got it! What is it?"

"Brian is the epitome of charm and thoughtfulness with clients," he said. "He should perform in the office in his *client-facing* character. He knows that character performance very well...so he just needs to bring it into the scenes of our office."

It worked like a charm. Or rather, "Charming Brian," which is what Brian became. He drew on that character and the view Charming Brian had of the world, and he used it with his officemates. He began relating to his colleagues and support staff as part of the client teams he worked with—which in fact they were. As his director, Liam helped Brian see, and be in, the larger play.

There are many varied and creative ways to access all of the wonderful and sometimes not-so-wonderful talent and resources in your midst—and it takes hard work. As Sam Mendes, the Oscar-winning director, says, "When you have a cast of twenty, this means you have twenty other imaginations in the room with you. Use them." And yes, it does put greater demands on you (*twenty people that I have to listen to?*) when you work creatively to support and connect and direct someone as who they are and who they could be. Sometimes it means being prescriptive and straightforward. Sometimes it means helping them to bring out a whole different part of themselves. As a coach/director, you're helping those you're coaching to perform a "head taller," as we've discussed before. And also as we've discussed, not a pinkie. Not three heads. One head taller. The creative challenge is figuring out how to get there together, by seeing, learning, and collaborating with your coachee. A small investment in directing can create growth, confidence, and results, as well as enhance the performance of the coachee, the coach, and the organization as a whole.

Coach as Theater Director Exercises

1. Creatively imitate a coach you admire: Who's a coach that you've had in your life (formally or informally) who has been especially helpful to you? Identify what she did and said. How did she talk to you? What kind of listener was she? What did she share of herself? Have her in mind as you work to direct and coach others. Creatively imitating people is not the same as stealing from them or being inauthentic. You'll be continuing to learn from them by adding some of their performances to yours.

2. If you have trouble being direct and straightforward, try this: For an upcoming feedback/coaching conversation, write yourself a script, be thoughtful about your language, and rehearse. Prepare for the emotional responses and impact that the feedback may trigger for both you and your coachee/performer:

   a) Come up with the opening line for what you need to speak with him about.

   b) Describe the situation and the impact of what he did or is doing.

   c) Articulate what you need for him to do differently.

3. Get to know the person you're coaching. Be curious, don't rush to solve any problems, and collaborate. Practice saying, "I don't know. Let's keep figuring this out together."

4. Give directions that are positive and specific. For example, rather than saying "Stop doing this," or "I'm looking for more engagement from you," try something like "Let's figure out two questions that you could ask in our next staff meeting. What do you want to know about the xyz project?"

5. Share your own struggles with growing and being directed/ coached. But be brief (don't pontificate!).

Epilogue

YOUR HANDY PERFORMANCE EXERCISE MANUAL

Acts II and III include exercises at the end of each chapter that are relevant to that chapter's theme. Now you're ready to move beyond the "themes," to mix and match your practice/rehearsal as you see fit. So here's a compilation—your "performance exercise manual." And to start it off, I've also provided a set of guidelines that apply to and will be helpful for virtually all of the new performance choices you will begin making in the varied scenes of your work and life. There are six of them, and when you put them together, they spell the acronym (what else?) BECOME:

Building the Stage
Emotional and Physical Preparation
Crafting New Scripts
Once Is Not Enough
Magic Time
Eye of the Director

Building the Stage

One of the most important factors in a conversation, presentation, or interaction is the physical environment. It's also one of the last things we usually consider. More often than not, we think it's not a big deal—the fourth-floor conference room should be okay for that meeting, the hallway or Starbucks will work for that conversation, or the dorky-looking podium in the ballroom at the off-site is what it is and can't be altered. To be sure, sometimes where you are is where you are and there's nothing to be done. But in our experience, that's true far less often than we think, so we need to attend to and work deliberately on shaping the stage/environment for the various performances in our work and life.

Emotional and Physical Preparation

Performing requires physical and emotional preparation. Actors, dancers, athletes, and improvisers understand this. How you stand, walk, and sit has an impact on both you and your audience; being attentive to how you're feeling is a crucial part of creating new performances that stretch you. Skilled performers are intentional and deliberate about the scene they are about to enter. They clear their minds and bodies of the scene in which they last performed, in order to be prepared and mindful about what is to come. Breath, body language, taking your emotional inventory, and other physical and emotional preparatory techniques don't just change how you walk into a room, they can transform how you work and live day-to-day.

Crafting New Scripts

It's amazing how having one new opening line in a scene can change everything. Or how a new script can prepare you for a colleague or boss who typically says things that you disagree with and that make you upset or throw you off balance in some way. The habitual scripts we use can produce unintended and undesired results, while new lines and scripts can pave the way for greater confidence and stronger relationships, better outcomes, and—in a fascinating performative paradox—can open the door to refreshing improvisational options and opportunities.

Once Is Not Enough

I'm a huge fan of rehearsing because it does double duty. On the one hand, rehearsing a play, a conversation, a song, a presentation, or a dance is important preparation for "the show," whatever form it takes. But rehearsing—especially in everyday work and life—is valuable for its own sake. Putting your performance-to-come "on its feet" is a performance unto itself and can be extraordinarily helpful in showing you what you know and don't know. Rehearsing creates new learning and produces new possibilities in real time.

Magic Time

Actors sometimes refer to the moment the show starts as "magic time." All the preparation and rehearsing is done, all the distractions from the rest of life fall away, and the amazing phenomenon of human beings performing something new begins. Sometimes it's a formal presentation, sometimes a conversation with a co-worker, sometimes a different way to talk to your kid. You're performing something new in front of an audience of one or many. And even when every bone in your body says, "I'm not the kind of person who does [fill-in-the-blank]," when the curtain goes up, now you are.

Eye of the Director

Both during rehearsals and after a show opens, actors get notes from their directors: *We couldn't hear your last line; the beginning of the kitchen scene hit exactly the right emotional tone—keep it; when you enter, make sure you have the prop chicken.* Directors' notes are an ongoing part of the process that helps performers to grow in their roles. Now remember that as a performer in life, you're not just *in* the scene/play, you're also a director. So what might typically be called reflecting, or debriefing, or taking stock, we at POAL call the "eye of the director." Whenever you've tried something new and changed your performance, it's crucial to take note of what happened— what went well, what didn't, what you learned, how you feel, and what to talk to others about—to help you continue to grow and move forward.

———

And now here are the exercises from the previous chapters all together. A reminder: Back in the prologue to this book, I brought up the idea of creating your own personal board of performance directors. If you haven't done that yet, now's the time. Many of the exercises that follow call for you to have somebody to work/play with. Your board need not be big (one or two people would work), and they don't need any special skills (although of course they can have special skills). Either way, they should be people you trust and who are open to—at least at first—simply joining you in some of the exercises. Though it's definitely not required, if they're interested in reading the book, too, that'd be great, because then you can be on *their* board.

Choose to Grow Exercises

1. Challenge the Knowing Paradigm by spending at least a day at work performing "not knowing." Make the choice to be uncertain, tolerant of ambiguity, and open, rather than having or even searching for an answer or explanation. Say things like, "I have no idea!," or "Let's sit with this for a while," or "There might not be a clear answer here."

2. Practice radical acceptance by thinking about something that a friend or colleague has brought up with you, or about you, that was difficult to hear and that you have rejected. Try it on for a while. Consider it as a possibility. See what you learn about yourself and what new performances you can create as a result.

3. Put yourself in a situation in which you have to do something that might make you say, "I couldn't possibly do that"—something you don't know how to do or you're not good at. Take a stab at a stretch assignment (e.g., volunteer for a project you wouldn't normally take on). Have a different kind of conversation than you typically have (e.g., give someone difficult feedback, ask for feedback, state a disagreement, or agree for a change).

Build Ensembles Everywhere Exercises

1. Create a ZPD. Bring people together to work on a project who have varied skills, are at different levels, and are different from one another in other ways. Talk about these differences and about your strengths and weaknesses, and work on your project, enthusiastically making use of all of it. Not clear what I mean? Not a problem. Figuring out how to do that together (i.e., deciding together what that means) is part of the ensemble-building process.

2. Spend a week using "we" every time you would normally say "I."

3. Put aside some time in a meeting, or with a friend, family member, or team, and ask the questions "How are we doing this together? Could we do this better? How do we think we're working and communicating together as a ____ (project team, department, marriage [!])." Don't rush to solve a problem or come up with a solution. Be focused on having the conversation—as an ensemble.

4. Be a casting director. Prepare for a meeting by thinking through what roles everyone might be able to play. Don't reserve this for "special occasions," such as project kickoffs or other new endeavors (but don't leave them out, either). Have a conversation together discussing who's doing what when and where, and how the ensemble wants to work together.

Listen!: The Revolutionary Way to Have a Conversation Exercises

1. Pick two meetings and a one-on-one conversation that are upcoming and choose to make listening your priority performance. Try not to listen *for* anything. Pause longer than you normally would before you respond. Make more eye contact than you usually do. Let people see that you are listening.

2. Take special notice of body language offers. How someone sits, her facial expressions, her walk, what she's looking at, and more. Listen, see, and respond to those offers.

3. Take someone else's point of view that you really disagree with. Spend some time—from fifteen minutes to a whole day—in his shoes, holding his opinions. How does he see the world? What do you see differently as a result?

4. Perform curiosity: Do you have a friend or colleague you disagree with about something? Have a conversation in which (for once!) you don't try to convince her she's wrong, but instead find out everything you can about how she sees the topic or issue. Don't assume you know anything.

5. Ask a colleague or friend to tell you a story about himself that you've never heard. Sit back and listen.

Create with Crap Exercises

1. The next time somebody says or does something that you think is stupid, irrelevant, or problematic, write a poem, draw a cartoon, or make up a song about it.

2. Following Professor Einstein's advice, bring a group of people together (your team, a few colleagues—or this could be a job for your personal board of performance directors) to "research" a toxic environment or situation at work—by playing with it. Create a short melodramatic play about it. Include scenes where you explore the mundane process—conversations, attitudes, decisions—that produced the crappy situation.

3. The next time you're having an argument with your significant other or a friend, ask him to dance instead.

4. Be on the lookout for the crap you're giving to others. Since we mostly think we're right, or that less-than-optimal things we do are justifiably in response to something else (which could very well be), it can be hard to see. But at least on a few occasions, notice your crap and then tell people, "I really did a bunch of crap today. Got any ideas about how to be creative with it?"

Improvise Your Life Exercises

1. Say **"Yes, and"** for an entire week at work and at home. Even if you don't say the words, listen carefully to what you hear (and see). Then, whatever you've perceived, say yes to it and then add something that accepts and builds with it. After you do this for a week, continue doing it for the rest of your life.

2. **Make 'em look good:** Help somebody out with a piece of work so that (1) she learns something; (2) the work gets better; and (3) she gets the credit. And for a bonus (not for you, but for someone else), in a meeting or two, respond to what someone says with the starting phrase "What I really like about what you said…"

3. Tell some colleagues about a doozy of a **mistake** you've made— today, yesterday, this year, in your life. Or open a meeting with it. Tell them you'd like them to applaud once they hear your mistake, and then

you take a bow. Ask people for their thoughts about what you and the organization might do to grow and learn from your mistake. Come up with real, specific ideas about this—not generalizations.

4. **Follow the follower:** Listen, respond, and follow someone (i.e., let him lead you) in a conversation, idea, or process when you might not typically do that. Let what he says and does affect what you say and do. See where you end up and what the experience of doing so is like.

5. Throw yourself a few **curveballs**. Make a decision without thinking it through carefully and thoroughly. Talk to someone at work you never talk with. Talk to a stranger and get into a philosophical conversation. When someone says or does something at work that throws you off balance, notice it. Smile and breathe. "Yes-and" it.

6. **Go into the cave:** Bring up an "elephant in the room" in a positive way. Ask someone about something personal that you know about but haven't really talked about. (Use your judgment about what's appropriate, of course.)

We're All Storytellers Exercises

1. Experiment with your own story: Introduce yourself at a networking event, a cocktail party, or a dinner—in new ways. Instead of simply saying your name and the usual stuff (where you work, what you do or your title, who you know, what you've done, etc.), include in your performance the words *I believe*, or *I've always thought*, or *I feel*. Use different lines with different people so that each conversation will be varied.

2. To begin "storifying" a business presentation, write/conceptualize/experiment with it by starting with the line "Once upon a time...," and taking it from there. Improviser/storyteller Kenn Adams's "Story Spine" expands on this idea, and to learn more, pick up the book *Training to Imagine* by Kat Koppett.

3. Tell a story to a friend and ask her to be your story director. Every time she wants to hear more details, she interrupts you and says, "Color," at which point you add color, such as *"The road was made of old cobblestones, which had been worn down by years of horses and then automobiles."* When your friend is satisfied with the detail, she interrupts and says, "Advance," and you continue the narrative of the story, such as *"And we*

took that road all the way to the restaurant in L'Orange where my adopted sister was waiting." And so on, with more coloring and more advancing.

4. Create/write/perform a story as three different characters. For example: Queen Elizabeth, Yoda, and your favorite colorful relative. Insist that a few friends sit around and listen. Invite them to do the same.

Those Challenging Conversations Exercises

1. Perform curiosity. Seek out somebody at work with whom you regularly disagree. Instead of an argument or dispute, have a conversation with him in which you're being curious and a learner the whole time. Feel free to review the rules of the curiosity exercise in chapter 5 on listening.

2. It's all about listening and hearing offers. Relate to everything that anybody says or does as an offer, with which you have both an opportunity and an obligation to create and build. Even and especially all of the crap. Fundamentally, let what's best for the relationship or project lead you.

3. The next time you have a conversation coming up that you're dreading, enlist the help of one of the members of your board of performance directors. Read this chapter together, and then tell her what the conversation is about and rehearse it with her. First have her play you, and respond to her with everything you dread hearing. Then have her play the person you need to talk to, and you play yourself.

The Art of Selling, Networking, and Other Schmoozy Things Exercises

1. Prepare for a conversation/scenario in which you usually would be trying to make a sale (or influence someone, or get him to do something). Perform with the sole intention of discovering what's important to him. Don't try to make a sale.

2. Before your next networking event, ask yourself: *What kind of scene/play is this event going to be? What characters can I expect to meet?* Then create a character and a particular performance for yourself. Examples to consider:

a) The Generous Host. You're there to make other people feel welcomed and comfortable.

b) The Most Curious Person. You've come to learn who people are, what they do, and what's important to them.

c) The Connector. Who are people you could introduce to one another? What connections can you offer to those you might meet in this context?

d) Your Role Model. Someone you know whose style of networking or selling you admire or think is effective.

3. Work with one of the members of your board of performance directors to come up with three different ways to introduce yourself and your product or service. Pay close attention to how people respond. What feels good to you and why? Learn what seems interesting to other people and what doesn't.

4. Hear offers, develop needs, see opportunities. Rinse and repeat.

Perform with Presence Exercises

Make use of your body and physicality—they are key factors for performing with presence:

1. Practice walking slowly and deliberately. Then stand still and relax. Do this as you walk around your office or workplace and when you are making a presentation.

2. Notice your posture—are you scrunched in any way, do you look down, hold on to yourself? Stand up straight and look around at people and the environment.

3. In your next presentation—whether to a group of five or five hundred—work to make eye contact with everyone. When you are speaking, look at specific people and allow yourself to finish a sentence while looking at one person.

4. Add silence to eliminate "um," "y'know," and the like. Rather than trying to stop saying "um" and "y'know," *add* silence and pauses instead.

Create your character with presence: Consider yourself the unofficial "host" of various meetings, gatherings, or conference/video calls.

Your job is to make other people feel comfortable and at ease, even if they are perfectly fine.

Experiment with different presence performances: Think of a story to tell or a short presentation to give. It doesn't have to be particularly interesting or dramatic; in fact, for this exercise it's better if it isn't. Tell it once the way you ordinarily would. (You'll need an audience for this—your personal board of performance directors, for example—or at a minimum a video of yourself doing it.) Now tell it again, with the addition of an *as if* direction. Then try another one. How did it feel to perform this material with the directions? What was the impact on the audience? Here are some sample directions, but feel free to make up your own (or ask your audience for suggestions):

- You're very excited about what you're talking about.
- You're addressing a kindergarten class.
- You're hung over.
- This information is top secret.
- You're madly in love with someone in the front row.

Coach as Theater Director Exercises

1. Creatively imitate a coach you admire: Who's a coach that you've had in your life (formally or informally) who has been especially helpful to you? Identify what she did and said. How did she talk to you? What kind of listener was she? What did she share of herself? Have her in mind as you work to direct and coach others. Creatively imitating people is not the same as stealing from them or being inauthentic. You'll be continuing to learn from them by adding some of their performances to yours.

2. If you have trouble being direct and straightforward, try this: For an upcoming feedback/coaching conversation, write yourself a script, be thoughtful about your language, and rehearse. Prepare for the emotional responses and impact that the feedback may trigger for both you and your coachee/performer:

    a) Come up with the opening line for what you need to speak with him about.

    b) Describe the situation and the impact of what he did or is doing.

    c) Articulate what you need for him to do differently.

3. Get to know the person you're coaching. Be curious, don't rush to solve any problems, and collaborate. Practice saying, "I don't know. Let's keep figuring this out together."

4. Give directions that are positive and specific. For example, rather than saying, "Stop doing this," or "I'm looking for more engagement from you," try something like "Let's figure out two questions that you could ask in our next staff meeting. What do you want to know about the xyz project?"

5. Share your own struggles with growing and being directed/coached. But be brief (don't pontificate!).

And last but not least, your new and final exercise:

MAKE UP YOUR OWN EXERCISES

An Inconclusive Conclusion

So here we are, at the end of *Performance Breakthrough*. The experience of writing it for you, dear reader, has been at times joyous and at times torturous. From beginning to end, I was performing as an author, doing what I didn't know how to do.

I hope that you've also begun performing who you are/who you are not yet. If so, you're now a full-fledged performer, actively making performance breakthroughs in your work and life. Your board of performance directors is a robust Zone of Proximal Development (don't worry, if you haven't formed one yet, you can do it now), and you and your various ensembles at work are exercising their ability to grow, to listen and build with offers, to create with crap, and to improvise in new and developmental ways. The Becoming Principle is alive in your actions, thoughts, and how you see yourself and others. So give yourself a round of applause! (You might want to go out to the parking lot first.)

Meanwhile, all the world's a stage.

There is a vibrant and growing community of people from all walks of life, all over the world (a big stage, indeed), who have discovered the power of performance as a transformative force. I am fortunate to have spent most of my adult life as part of it, and now you are, too. Performance breakthroughs—the use of performance to create breakthroughs and the enhanced performance that results—are happening in some of the most unlikely places you might imagine. Here are just a few of those places and people who make up your performance community:

• The Hunter Heartbeat Method was founded by Kelly Hunter, an actor with the Royal Shakespeare Company, as a way to work with children with a diagnosis on the autism spectrum. Shakespeare's iambic pentameter rhythm of speech mimics the sound of a heartbeat, which calms the children and allows them to feel safe to communicate. And Shakespeare's themes provide them with a way into otherwise inaccessible imaginative and emotional worlds. Using games that play with plot and themes that emphasize the eyes, mind, and heart, children with a diagnosis on the spectrum experiment with performances of intense emotions (jealousy, love, ambition, anger), which are an essential part of the Shakespeare canon.

• Actor, director, and writer Alan Alda has been a lifelong science promoter and enthusiast. While hosting the TV show *Scientific American Frontiers*, he began to notice how difficult it was for scientists to speak about their work to nonscientists—dry technical lecturing rather than personal conversation, ordinary language, and stories. Alda wondered why we can't train scientists to be good communicators while we train them to be scientists. Nobody had a good answer, so in 2009 he helped found the Alan Alda Center for Communicating Science at Stony Brook University. Using improv games and techniques, Alda helps scientists develop their listening and interpersonal skills so they can learn to connect with other people and speak about their work in a more immediate and engaging way. As more effective communicators, scientists can share ideas—with the public, with policy makers, with other researchers outside their discipline, and even (as Alda wryly observes) with their grandmothers. The result? Better understanding of important scientific discoveries, trends, and solutions; more informed policy decisions; and—through increased cross-disciplinary collaboration—better science.

• In 2001, psychology professor Tom Verner was traveling through Eastern Europe when he stopped off at refugee camps in Kosovo and Macedonia to share his passion: magic. The amateur magician received such a strong response that he took a leave from teaching and started performing full-time. The result: Magicians Without Borders, a nonprofit organization run by Verner and his wife, artist and teacher Janet Fredericks. Performing magic shows in more than thirty countries, primarily in refugee camps, orphanages, and hospitals—places scarred by war and tragedy and desperately in need of laughter and magic—the organization has entertained an estimated half a million individuals, using the joy of magic to touch the lives of young people around the world. And in

El Salvador, India, and Colombia, Magicians Without Borders is training children to become magicians, empowering them to imagine a life that veers from the sadly typical path of gang violence, sex work, and poverty.

• Olie Westheimer has been running a dance workshop program for people with Parkinson's disease in Brooklyn in collaboration with the Mark Morris Dance Group since 2001. A former dancer, Olie worked with Mark Morris dancers to develop a regular class for Parkinson's patients, incorporating elements of traditional dance and encouraging spontaneous choreography and improvisation. Just as singing can help stutterers speak smoothly, dance's ability to integrate physical, mental, and emotional elements of movement helps people with Parkinson's move their bodies in a new way and allows them to relate to one another not as patients, or recipients of care, but as dancers, as students—regular people socializing and having a good time.

• Twenty-five students, ages twenty to thirty, enter the room of an ESL (English as a second language) American literature college class in midtown Manhattan. They have all recently arrived in the United States from every country imaginable and barely speak a word of English. They're nervous, soft-spoken, apprehensive. Their teacher, Gwen Lowenheim, instructs them to put their coffee and book bags aside and gather in a circle. They begin passing an imaginary ball to one another, following strange rules that include saying "Whoosh" when they pass to their right or left, "Whoa!" when they don't want the ball, "Zap" to pass it across the circle, and "Freak out!" when they run around the room waving their arms in the air. Within moments they're all speaking a shared language—a few simple words and the all-important language of laughter. Lowenheim builds on this playful, performative environment, casting the students in improvisational plays where they practice the English used in classic American literature. It doesn't feel like school. It feels like play. They perform as English speakers before they know how, and they become speakers of English in the process.

• For more than a decade, thousands of performance activists from around the world have gathered at the biannual international conference Performing the World, initially convened by developmental psychologist Lois Holzman, whom you met earlier. These activists are academics, doctors, business executives, visual artists, psychologists, theater directors, actors, performance artists, educators, social workers, youth workers, health-care professionals, organizational consultants, students, scientists, and architects, and they hail from more than fifty countries. Using performance in the most creative ways imaginable, they tackle some of the most difficult issues in our world: illiteracy, physical and mental abuse, political corruption, environmental disasters, displaced refugees, children living on the streets, HIV/AIDS, and more. Through performance they are building community, changing lives, and helping people to see and create possibility and opportunity.

• In partnership with the Cognitive Neurology and Alzheimer's Disease Center (CNADC) at Northwestern University in Chicago, the Lookingglass Theatre created the Memory Ensemble: An Improvisational Theater Experience for People with Memory Loss. This eight-week program for people with early-stage Alzheimer's employs improvisation because it allows a fully involved performance experience without relying on scripts or memorization. And there is "no experience necessary"—given that all human beings improvise all the time, the participants are, in fact, experienced. For most, it's one of the only activities in which they're not talking about their problems or difficulties with Alzheimer's. They are playing, laughing, learning something new, and living life, with others.

• For the past decade, developmental psychologist and activist Lenora Fulani has produced Operation Conversation: Cops & Kids, a program sponsored by the nonprofit All Stars Project. This grassroots innovation uses performance and improvisation to help create conversations and build a bridge between a usually hostile pairing: police officers and teenagers of color from the inner city. Cut to the world-famous Apollo Theater in Harlem, New York, where 800 newly graduated New York City police officers and 650 civilians of all races, ages, genders, and social strata gather to watch a demonstration workshop of the program. Onstage, six officers and six young people move in slow motion, synchronize their hand claps, and perform improvised skits. Interspersed between these explicitly theatrical segments, they perform a conversation that touches on how an inner-city teenager and a police officer are two of the hardest things to be. They discover that many of them on both sides worry that when they leave home in the morning they might not ever see their families again. They share with one another the worst thing that has happened to them. They listen and say things that they have never uttered to the other: "I'm sorry that this happened to you." At the end they shake hands, or hug. They see one another as people for the first time.

This book has been all about helping you to create the scenes of your workplace and your life. It's been about performing as a method to help you make performance breakthroughs and become who you are not... yet. Call me crazy, but I believe that performance is also a method for creating our world. Anew. There are a lot of new scenes to create out there! It will involve us all being who we are/who we are not, together. In fact, I think that this is the only way we can do it. Being only who we are means everything stays the same. Being who we're not? Well... who's to say what new play we can create together?

> For here, I hope, begins our lasting joy.
> —*William Shakespeare,* Henry VI, *part 3*

Acknowledgments, Appreciation, and Applause

There would be no book without Jim Levine, Arielle Eckstut, David Henry Sterry, David Nackman, Lois Holzman, Drew Dernavich, and the wonderful folks at Hachette Books.

Jim, my agent, guided me throughout the entire process, starting by passionately confirming and convincing me that *Performance Breakthrough* should be written. A believer in the power of performance well before he met me, Jim practiced what I preached, and he gave it back to me with wisdom, creativity, compassion, humor, and wit. He was at times my director, my role-play partner, my therapist, my friend, and my wordsmith. I feel like I hit the jackpot with him (I'm sure he hopes he hit the jackpot with me). And whenever the writing got tough, he promised me that there was a golf outing (with him) in my future. That always kept me motivated.

Arielle Eckstut and David Henry Sterry, the amazing "Book Doctors" (thebookdoctors.com), gave me their heart and soul along with their years of experience in writing, acting, improvisation, coaching, and publishing. Their enthusiasm, humor, brains, passion, and creativity were constant, and I will treasure working with them always. Writing can be a lonely activity done in solitude. With Arielle and David I never felt alone.

David Nackman has been my creative and business partner for twenty years, building Performance of a Lifetime together from day one. I first saw him onstage on Broadway in the Neil Simon play *Broadway Bound*, and I was starstruck. And intimidated. He had so much talent, verve, verbosity, and intelligence packed into such a little guy. I managed to work through my initial intimidation so that we could work together, and "the rest is history." One of our most recent projects has been working on

Performance Breakthrough. A master storyteller and wit, he made everything better, sharper, and cleaner. Sometimes we argued and sometimes we guffawed and sometimes we cried and sometimes we hugged. With David by my side, I knew this project was possible; we would get there.

Lois Holzman has been a mentor, colleague, and friend for more than thirty years. You've met her in the pages of this book already; she is the director of a postmodern training center and think tank, the East Side Institute (eastsideinstitute.org), and the author of numerous academic books and a popular blog on *Psychology Today.* Lois read each chapter carefully and thoughtfully—I think she read the book as many times as I did. She was both my favorite critic (oh boy, she's a straight shooter) and my favorite fan. Her intellectual and methodological challenges made me and the book smarter. She delighted when I made a discovery, and she pushed and wouldn't settle when mediocrity or confusion crept in. Her e-mails ranged from "Let's speak" (yikes) to "Awesome" (really?) and always gave me confidence and joy... eventually.

"*Woo-hoo!*"

I first met Drew Dernavich in 2011 at an innovation conference where he and his *New Yorker* cartoonist colleagues were doing an improvisational performance of creating cartoons based on suggestions from the audience. I was mesmerized by his talent, wit, and pathos. It took several years for me to come up with a project that we could do together, and now you're looking at it. Drew understood and "got" *Performance Breakthrough* right away. His artwork is an improvisational response (his "Yes, and") that has made the book that much more interesting, accessible, and meaningful. Thank you, Drew, for such a special collaboration. I can't imagine the book without it.

Heartfelt thanks to the amazing people at Hachette. Mauro DiPreta, my publisher, took a chance with me by inviting me to be part of his first coterie of authors in his new imprint, Hachette Books. Mauro, thank you for your enthusiasm and passion for this project. The gods were smiling down at me when they gave me such an awesome editor as Stacy Creamer. From the beginning, Stacy, you asked great questions and challenged me to think harder and more holistically throughout the whole process. Deborah Wiseman was my sharp-eyed copy editor, and production editor Carolyn Kurek was as careful and thoughtful as could be. Betsy Hulsebosch and Michelle Aielli were always on the case with their marketing and PR magic. And Lauren Hummel kept everything moving along, with grace and on schedule.

Okay. Think Golden Globes—the orchestra is beginning to play, and I'm just getting warmed up. I have many more people to thank, both for the book and for Performance of a Lifetime.

Maureen Kelly is a friend and colleague like no other. She has trusted me in ways that no one else has. She trusted me enough to leave a very well paying job at a big bank to join POAL. She trusted me enough to join with a community of activists, thinkers, artists, educators, psychologists; poor, rich, and middle-class people who are crazy enough to think we can change the world. She trusted me enough to go on very badly planned vacations. She trusted me to write about her amazing work with clients, and she gave me excellent and much-needed input on the book. She trusted me to be part of her extended family, which includes her partner—the talented and kind Andrew Carbone—and their ridiculously adorable and intelligent son, Henry. Without Maureen, I would not have felt that POAL could withstand my leave of absence to write this book. But she pushed me out the door. "Do this for us!" she insisted. Performance of a Lifetime is safe, sound, and soaring...because of her. I hope she lets me back into the office.

Sevanne Kassarjian is a total delight to work, talk, and play with. If I didn't have to work for a living, I'd like to follow her around all the time.

She's been a major contributor to POAL as it has continued to evolve, bringing a depth of intelligence, intensity, curiosity, passion, and love to all that she touches. Her thoughtful and eagle eye on the book was always helpful and clarifying.

I first met Bobby Greenberg when he was a POAL client, heading a marketing team at a global insurance company. I remember thinking to myself, *Jeez, I guess POAL would have to be a really big company to ever get such a smart and ambitious guy like him to work for us.* Well, I lucked out. Eventually we got Bobby, and he has been our secret weapon, guiding us to be big enough and bad enough for him to work for.

Other awesome people on the POAL team: Super talented and hard-working designer, trainer, and improviser Bradford Jordan makes everything seem easy; I love having him around when he's not out doing kickass client work in Hong Kong or Munich or Amsterdam, and I'm not in Dallas, Columbus, or Pittsburgh...Wait a minute—who's deciding the gig assignments?

Tisse Takagi is all you could ask for in a research assistant. One of the most can-do people I know, she could and did do it all. Quotes, far-flung research, fact checks, fetching clothes for photo shoots, interview transcribing, finding lost files, helpful opinions, you name it, she did it, with ease, capability, and a sense of humor.

Thanks to Kris Cheppaikode for your ability to navigate all the details and moving parts as you cheerfully move scores of POAL trainers to where they need to be, on time and knowing what they're supposed to do. Helen Poon, our CFO—your keeping POAL organized and solvent lets me sleep well at night.

To the magnificent POAL core team of trainers: Bobbi Block, Melissa Delaney-del Valle, Simon Dowling, Jeff Flowers, Adam Grupper, Kat Koppett, Carol Noakes, Shannon Polly, Corinna Powlesland, Brenny Rabine, and Patti Stiles. You have taken the Becoming Principle places I never imagined. You inspire me, educate me, and humble me. Thank you.

To the wonderful POAL training team over the years—too many to mention without inadvertently leaving somebody out. Beth Adler, Andy Allis, Karmann Bajuyo, Pun Bandhu, Purva Bedi, Renee Bergeron, Judy Blue, Suellen Burton, Hilary Chaplain, Madelyn Chapman, Dave DeChristopher, Scott Faris, Jim Farruggio, Dion Flynn, Chris Grace, Daniel Guerra, Sam Guncler, Ricardo Gutierrez, Cheryl Hamada, Steven

Hart, Torsten Hillhouse, Diana Hird, Jamie Johnson, Deep Katdare, Dev Kennedy, Mmakgosi Kgabi, Sean Kwan, Nina Kwok, Gwen Lowenheim, Stuart Luth, Holly Mandel, Terry Milner, Neela Muñoz, Rozz Nash, Sian Palmer, Deb Rabbai, Jay Rhoderick, Jamie Roach, Michael Rock, Catherine Hanna Schrock, Warona Seane, Richard Shavzin, Nandita Shenoy, Colin Skelton, Greg Skura, Jeff Smithson, Stephan Spencer, Nate Starkey, Cheryl Stern, Daniel Sullivan, Anne Thibault, and Genevieve Ven Johnson. You are the real deal—terrific performers with heads and hearts who have helped thousands of people every year become who they are not yet.

Thank you to our wonderful and innovative clients, who across their broad range of industries, geographies, and sizes have taken the creative plunge with POAL and taught us so much in the process.

A special thank-you to Gabrielle Kurlander, president and CEO of the All Stars Project, for the work you do bringing performance for growth and development to inner-city youth across America. And thank you to the All Stars' talented staff, thousands of volunteers, board of directors, and the young people and their families who every day find new and creative ways to perform their lives, their communities, and our collective future. The All Stars vision is a big part of why I do what I do, and I only hope that POAL can continue to make a bigger and bigger contribution toward that vision.

To the Proverbial Loons ensemble at the Castillo Theatre: my fellow improvisers with a heart Olivia Hartle, Ava Jenkins, David Nackman, J. B. Opdyke, Andy Parker, John Rankin III, Marian Rich, and Frank Spitznagel. Playing with all of you reminds me that while improvising in everyday life is essential, improvising onstage is a total blast.

Deep gratitude to Lenora Fulani, developmental psychologist, cofounder of All Stars, creator of Operation Conversation: Cops & Kids. Not a day goes by when I don't think about your groundbreaking work in building bridges between people who "don't belong" together. Black and white, rich and poor, cops and kids, liberals and conservatives, and on and on. And you've been there for me personally, throughout the good and the bad, with your special brand of love and toughness. Thank you for supporting me in so many ways while I worked on this book, including our wonderful conversations about performance, power, and authenticity.

Thank you to Dan Pink, who embraced my work enthusiastically after our chance meeting on a gig together. Thank you for our many fascinating conversations and for including our work in your wonderful book *To Sell Is Human*. I'm honored to be in your company, and I feel passionately that your writing and insights have made and continue to make an important difference in the world.

To Sheila Heen of the Triad Consulting Group and coauthor of *Difficult Conversations* and *Thanks for the Feedback*. If there were fairy godmothers, Sheila would be mine. I'd always admired her, but from afar. She embraced me and this book beyond what I could have hoped for, gave me thoughtful, concrete, and actionable feedback, and coached me on everything from environment to punctuation to style to voice to content. Thank you, Sheila, for your friendship and high standards.

And speaking of fairy godmothers, the "power chicks"—an amazing group of women authors and leaders—appeared in my life at just the right time. Christine Bader, Jennifer Garvey Berger, Susan Cain, Amy Cuddy, Erica Ariel Fox, and Sheila Heen inspired me and provided the moral support and wisdom that made me believe that yes, I could actually do this.

Carrie Lobman, assistant professor at Rutgers University and author of several books on play and performance, was a friend and champion throughout. Our conversations about Vygotsky, authenticity, and the best coffee shops to write in were essential to the book. And my dear friend, educator Gwen Lowenheim, patiently listened to sections that weren't ready for human consumption with enthusiasm and helpful feedback. She photographed the writing journey during our late Tuesday night get-togethers and was always up for a wild dance around my apartment to celebrate the completion of a paragraph.

For reading early and late versions of the book and sharing most important feedback, deep appreciation goes to Edward Barnes, Ed Brady, Mary Fridley, Nancy Green, Bobby Greenberg, Adam Grupper, Lori Hanau, Sheila Heen, Chris Helm, Bradford Jordan, Sevanne Kassarjian, Maureen Kelly, Jim Kochalka, Carrie Lobman, Gwen Lowenheim, Marian Rich, Scott Ritter, Judy Rosenblum, Jacqueline Salit, Murray Salit, Doug Stone, and Doug White.

I owe a debt to the Business Writers Boot Camp crew, led by Sheila Heen and Doug Stone. Bob Bordone, Stevenson Carlebach, Mooly Dinnar, Jonno Hanafin, Joe Houde, Elaine Lin, Bob Reinheimer, Jim Tull, and Bauback Yeganeh—our week in Newport in the bitter cold was inspirational, instructive, supportive, and provided the push I needed to really roll up my sleeves and write. Watch for their books when they come out! They're going to be great.

Barb O'Neill and Carrie Lobman's book *Play and Performance* provided me with rich material on performance work around the globe. Ken Gergen, psychology professor emeritus at Swarthmore College, gave me important insights in his book *Relational Being.* The writings and spoken words of Patch Adams, Dan Ariely, Alan Arkin, Mary Catherine Bateson, Augusto Boal, James Carse, Jim Collins, Carol Dweck, Dan Friedman, Atul Gawande, Bonny Gildin, Sheila Heen, Lois Holzman, Keith Johnstone, Stephen King, Kat Koppett, Anne Lamott, Judith Malina, Patricia Ryan Madson, Rafael Méndez, Fred Newman, Alva Noë, Marge Piercy, Daniel Pink, Keith Sawyer, Viola Spolin, Sir Ken Robinson, Mark Rylance, Doug Stone, Ben Zander, and Rosamund Stone Zander all inspired, guided, educated, touched, reminded, and helped make *Performance Breakthrough* the book that it is.

My dear friend, attorney and poet Alvaader Frazier, was an important source of love, energy, and support as I wrote. Thank you, Alvaader, for more than a few late-night phone calls when you were exactly the person I needed to speak to.

Nancy Green co-founded POAL with Fred, David, and me, and is one of my oldest and dearest friends. Love often comes with mistakes and pain; thank you for reaching out your hand and grabbing mine.

I met Judy Rosenblum in 2001 when she was chief operating officer of the long-standing number one ranked custom executive education firm, Duke Corporate Education. We began a conversation about learning, development, business, and life that has been nonstop ever since. Judy and I love to work together—to design, teach, create, hatch plans, deconstruct, experiment. We also love to hang out and talk endlessly, and we never seem to get enough of it. Thank you for all of the guidance, love, and support you've given me before, and of course during, the writing of this book.

My beautiful friend and colleague Christine LaCerva is one of those people who make you want to be as creative as you can be, possibly because she is just so damn talented and creative herself. Thank you for all of your caring, humor, and wisdom. I would not have been able to write this book, and do all that came before it that set the stage, without your love and support.

Thank you to my wonderful friends for being there in my life, work, and throughout the writing of this book in so many different ways: Jeff Aron, Doug Balder, Madelyn Chapman, Joyce Dattner, Sandy Friedman, Mary Fridley, Bonny Gildin, Lori Hanau, Chris Helm, Cary Hirschfield, June Hirsh, Jim Horton, Emilie Knoerzer, Jim Kochalka, Kat Koppett, Harry Kresky, Warren Liebesman, Lisa Linnen, Jessica Massad, Melissa Meyer, Elizabeth Newman, Gail Peck, Betsi Pendry, Hugh Polk, Marian Rich, Nancy Ross, Cathy Stewart, Diane Stiles, Chris Street, Andrew Tatarsky, Lisa Vertucci, Pat Wagner, Michael Walsh, and Janet Wootten.

Martha Greene let me live a writer's dream by allowing me to use her beautiful home near the beach. Edward Barnes watched out for me and Otis throughout, making life just a bit easier and manageable as a result. Javier Dzul kept me physically strong and flexible with his shaman-like guidance of gyrotonics and head- and handstands. Violet Zaki kicked my ass with her special blend of martial arts and sensitivity.

Rod Borrie came into my life when the book project was almost done. There I was, immersed in an intense, expansive, fascinating, passionate, and all-encompassing experience, only to be surprised with another one—you. Thank you for opening your heart and your family to me.

A big thank-you and shout-out to colleagues and clients for the many conversations, interviews, e-mails, texts, and letters that helped me write the book: Chuck Alsdorf, Erika Andersen, Mary Catherine Bateson, David Belmont, Jesse Broome, Karen Davis, Howard Edelbaum, Dion Flynn, Marc Gerald, Dan Graf, Bobby Greenberg, Adam Grupper, Chris Helm, Sharon Krumm, Christine LaCerva, Warren Liebesman, Gwen Mandell, Sean McDowell, Carrie Sackett, Brian Saluzzo, Jonathan Schuldenfrei, Stuart Sears, Phil Terry, Andrew Valmon, Scott Wahlstrom, and Janet Wootten.

Thank you to the generous professional colleagues who have schooled me in the world of executive education. I'm sure to miss many, but to name at least a few: Lauren Ashwell, Sigall Bell, Ann Bohara, Nedra Bradsher, Michael Canning, Michael Chavez, Terry Dillon, Tom Evans, Mark Frein, Pete Gerend, Rick Gilkey, Hope Greenfield, Russ Hamilton, Courtney Harrison, Steven Hart, Leah Houde, Mark Hurst, Jerrilou Johnson, Sean Kavanagh, Ken Kesslin, Jim Kochalka, Pat Longshore, Steve Mahaley, John Malitoris, Alicia Mandel, Susan Massad, Patrick McLaurin, Gil McWilliam, Liz Mellon, Jeff Mitchell, Maureen Monroe, Alyce Mumbuchi, Blair Sheppard, Candice Sherman, Sandra Shullman, David Gary Smith, Keisha Smith-Jeremie, Cheryl Stokes, Kim Taylor-Thompson, Lisa Vertucci, Lisa Wardle, and Randy White.

Thank you to AIN, the Applied Improvisation Network, a vibrant community of teachers, educators, and facilitators who push the boundaries on the use of improvisation everywhere. So many people: Nan Crawford, Karen Dawson, Izzy Gesell, Gary Hirsch, Julie Huffaker, Paul Jackson, Caitlin McClure, Viv McWaters, Denzil Meyers, Johnnie Moore, Alain Rostain, Gary Schwartz, Brad Robertson, and Thiagi and are among these special peeps.

To the thousands of performance activists around the world, from Nairobi to Belgrade to São Paolo to Copenhagen to Hyderabad to Bedford-Stuyvesant to Taipei to Calgary to Johannesburg to London to Melbourne, who have shared their work and their passion as part of the biannual Performing the World conference (performingtheworld .org): Your experience, talent, commitment, and vision to changing the world—performing it anew—keep me fueled and inspired.

And to my family:

My mother, Sema Salit, who passed away from cancer in 1992, was and remains one of my biggest inspirations. You met her in the introduction, and you may have thought, *Wow, what an amazing woman*. She sure was. And she sure is. When I demonstrate a one-minute performance of a lifetime in a workshop, more often than not I perform something that includes my mom. That way more and more people get to meet her, and I get to spend time with her again. Sema, you are with me every day.

I love my father, Murray Salit, like nobody's business. And speaking of business, he instilled a driving, working-class ambition and entrepreneurship in me that makes me jump out of bed in the morning ready to work, live, and fight if necessary. He's still so proud of his junior high school dropout daughter who done good. And that still helps me stand just a little taller. Thank you for your unconditional love and support and for cheering me on—every single step of the way.

Jackie Salit, my brilliant and beautiful sister. Wow, JS. We're both published authors. Who'da thunk it? But seriously, *you are my hero*. And you are many people's hero. The world is a more hopeful and smarter place because of you, and I couldn't be more proud, happy, and lucky to be living my life with you. And as always, you were right there whenever I needed you, navigating the publishing world, discussing influencing without authority, or making me a vodka gimlet. Thank you for giving me the support—and the space—to write *Performance Breakthrough*.

Susan Salit, I am deeply saddened that you will not be able to read this book. As Jackie said at your graveside once you finally succumbed after a six-year battle with cancer, you were not our mother from blood, but you were our mother from love. Thank you for your bottomless support, your grace, and your big heart. And thank you for loving my father and making him so happy.

Joshua Salit and David Abramson, my two brothers, with whom I share love, joy, and sadness together and all at once, you are wonderful, caring men. Thank you for taking such good care of Susan and Murray in all of the incredible ways that you did. We lost Susan right at the completion of this book. It hurt so much. My pain was tempered only by being with both of you throughout it all.

My final thank-you is saved for the philosopher, political activist, playwright, director, therapist, author, social entrepreneur, improviser, and friend, Fred Newman. If it weren't for you, Fred, I wouldn't have anything to write about. The thousands and thousands of people and organizations that POAL has helped would not have been the beneficiary of this magnificent breakthrough of performance methodology. But there was you. And the world is a better place because of that. And I'll keep keepin' on, to try to make it better for more people. Thank you, Fred. For giving me a performance of a lifetime.

Recommended Reading

Alan Arkin, *An Improvised Life: A Memoir* (Da Capo, 2011).

A retrospective by the Academy Award–winning actor, including stories of his time at Second City in Chicago and on Broadway, highlighting the powerful influence of improvisation on the course of his acting and his life.

Mary Catherine Bateson, *Composing a Life* (Grove Press, 2001).

A reflection on the idea of life as an improvisational art form, as told through the lives of five highly productive and successful women: Joan Erikson, Alice d'Entremont, Ellen Bassuk, Johnnetta Cole, and the author herself.

James P. Carse, *Finite and Infinite Games: A Vision of Life as Play and Possibility* (Free Press, 1986).

Exploring the distinction between finite games (played to win) and infinite games (played to continue the play), this rich work of intellectual play teases apart complex subjects such as sex, culture, and religion.

Harold Clurman, *On Directing* (Fireside, 1997).

An insightful consideration of the job of a theatrical director by one of the most influential directors and drama critics of our time, including Clurman's own directing notes for ten of his best-known productions.

Kenneth J. Gergen, *Relational Being: Beyond Self and Community* (Oxford University Press, 2011).

To counter the tyranny of Enlightenment individualism, a psychologist introduces the concept of relational being. Arguing that we exist in a world of co-creation, he shows that we can only understand ourselves through our relationships with others.

Adam Grant, *Give and Take: Why Helping Others Drives Our Success* (Penguin, 2014).

Most of us operate as takers, matchers, or givers, according to the Wharton

School's youngest tenured professor, who gives us a fascinating examination of why being a giver—without expecting anything in return—might be the greatest way to achieve success.

Lois Holzman, *Vygotsky at Work and Play* (Routledge, 2008).

A wide-ranging study of Vygotskian methodologies at work in developmental and learning contexts, including Performance of a Lifetime.

Herminia Ibarra, *Act Like a Leader, Think Like a Leader* (Harvard Business Review Press, 2015).

Turning the leadership dictum "think first, then act" on its head, an INSEAD professor shows that people start thinking like leaders by doing leadership work. By prioritizing experience over thought, her three rules help to develop leaders from the outside in.

Kelly Leonard and Tom Yorton, *Yes, And: How Improvisation Reverses "No, But" Thinking and Improves Creativity and Collaboration—Lessons from The Second City* (HarperBusiness, 2015).

The wonderful Second City troupe specializes in helping businesses incorporate improv techniques into their workplaces and business practices.

Kat Koppett, *Training to Imagine: Practical Improvisational Theatre Techniques for Trainers and Managers to Enhance Creativity, Teamwork, Leadership, and Learning* (Stylus, 2012).

A practical guidebook, by one of applied improvisation's earliest innovators, that shows how we can start using applied improvisation in our work and in our lives.

Liz Lerman, *Hiking the Horizontal: Field Notes from a Choreographer* (Wesleyan, 2011).

A collection of autobiographical essays by a MacArthur "Genius" choreographer, examining dance as a vehicle for human insight and understanding of the world around us.

Doug Lipman, *Improving Your Storytelling: Beyond the Basics for All Who Tell Stories in Work or Play* (August House Publishers, 1999).

A practical framework and guide for improving your storytelling skills by a professional storyteller and teacher.

Brian McDonald, *Invisible Ink: A Practical Guide to Stories That Resonate* (Libertary, 2010).

An award-winning screenwriter reveals the secrets of the storytelling—and screenwriting—craft, highlighting the importance of the "invisible ink" that brings to life the "visible ink" on the page.

Stephen Nachmanovitch, *Free Play: Improvisation in Life and Art* (G. P. Putnam's Sons, 1991).

A brilliant meditation on improvisation in life and how to unleash the joy of creation and our inherent creative energy, by a violinist and educator.

Fred Newman, *Performance of a Lifetime: A Practical-Philosophical Guide to the Joyous Life* (Castillo International, 1996).

Philosopher Fred Newman teaches non-philosophers how to engage in the activity of philosophizing—what he calls asking big questions about little things. Through practical example, *Performance of a Lifetime* shows how appreciating the banal and the magic of everyday life can be a profoundly joyous experience.

Daniel H. Pink, *To Sell Is Human: The Surprising Truth About Moving Others* (Riverhead, 2013).

The book on the art and science of sales. Dan Pink's illuminating work shows that whether we're in consulting, education, or small business, what we're really doing is selling.

Ken Robinson, *Out of Our Minds: Learning to Be Creative*, rev. ed. (Capstone, 2011).

In today's quickly changing world, Robinson argues, we need more than ever to cultivate and promote creativity in education, business, and as a way of thinking.

Keith Sawyer, *Group Genius: The Creative Power of Collaboration* (Basic Books, 2008).

A fascinating book on collective creativity that convincingly debunks the myth of the solitary genius and explains how to create fertile creative conditions for any ensemble.

Viola Spolin, *Improvisation for the Theater* (Northwestern University Press, 1963).

The original improv handbook, written by the mother of improvisational theater, this book features hundreds of games that inspired the work of everyone from Upright Citizens Brigade to us at POAL.

Douglas Stone, Bruce Patton, and Sheila Heen, *Difficult Conversations: How to Discuss What Matters Most* (Penguin, 2010).

Three of the sharpest minds from the Harvard Law School and the Harvard Negotiation Project help us peer beneath the surface and see the nuts and bolts of difficult conversations so we can move on from blame to productive solutions.

Rosamund Stone Zander and Benjamin Zander, *The Art of Possibility: Transforming Professional and Personal Life* (Penguin Books, 2002).

A book filled with moving stories and ideas about change and transformation as a creative, artistic human activity.

Twyla Tharp, *The Creative Habit: Learn It and Use It for Life* (Simon & Schuster, 2003).

Creativity is not a gift from the gods, says Twyla Tharp, bestowed by some divine and mystical spark. It is the product of preparation and effort, and it's within reach of everyone who wants to achieve it.

Index

About the Author

CATHY SALIT is the CEO of Performance of a Lifetime, a singer, an actor, and an artistic associate at the Castillo Theatre in New York City. She is a speaker, facilitator, executive coach, instructional designer, and social entrepreneur. Cathy performs regularly with the musical improv comedy troupe the Proverbial Loons and, less frequently, sings jazz and R & B on any stage she can find or create. She lives in New York City.

About the Illustrator

DREW DERNAVICH is an award-winning cartoonist who has taken his passion for art and communication and applied it across a myriad of creative endeavors, including gravestone engraving, graphic recording, and authoring the children's book *It's Not Easy Being the Number Three*. He has been a regular cartoonist for *The New Yorker* since 2002 and has also drawn cartoons for Google, *TIME*, *The Wall Street Journal*, *Harvard Business Review*, and the *Boston Globe*. Drew lives in New York City.

About Performance of a Lifetime

Performance of a Lifetime (POAL) is a consulting firm that helps leaders, teams, and organizations grow their business by focusing on the human side of strategy. Using the art and science of performance, we help leaders close the gap between the status quo and their desired future. Our team of coaches and human development experts leverage our proprietary method, The Becoming Principle™, to engage leaders and entire organizations in discovering, creating, and acting on new and uncharted possibilities. Our services include organizational change solutions, custom leadership development programs, professional development workshops, and individual and team coaching.

POAL is headquartered in New York City with teams across the globe. Our clients include Nike, DIRECTV, News Corp, Chanel, American Express, PwC, Rolls-Royce, Coca-Cola, Johns Hopkins Hospital, Grey Group, and Bank of America. Our work has been featured in best-selling author Daniel Pink's *To Sell Is Human* and on the pages of *The Wall Street Journal*, *BusinessWeek*, *Wired*, and *Fast Company*.

Learn more at www.performanceofalifetime.com.